C000226349

Vincent has the rare talent of understanding the power of emotional connection and business opportunity to serve diverse markets. He has led many companies down a practical road that achieved immediate results and long-term success. This book is a great guide to a world that's changed and is still changing.

—**CHUCK KAVITSKY**,
former CEO of Allianz of America

As a thirty-two-year-old firm providing diversity, equity, and inclusion assessment and strategy services, we've been fortunate to work with some truly great executives. Leaders that understood the tremendous opportunity that diversity and inclusion represented to world-class organizations. Vince is one of those executives. Working with corporate clients more than twenty years ago, we predicted that demographic changes would radically transform the workforce, workplace, and marketplace. The future is now. Vince's book is a must-read to understand how to attract, capture, and serve today's diverse marketplace.

—**JANET & GARY SMITH**, IVY Planning

The growth of the financial services industry will be driven by having more diverse advisors serving diverse communities across the country. Vince is a respected leader who has helped open the eyes of many leaders in the industry to the opportunities that multicultural markets present.

—**KEVIN MAYEUX**, CEO of NAIFA

Diversity Means Dollars is a must-read for leaders in the financial industry. Vince is a leading figure in developing strategies for your business to attract advisors and clients that mirror the exploding diversity of US demographics.

—**HARRY HOOPIS**, Chairman of Hoopis Performance Network

Diversity Means Dollars, written by Vince Vitiello, is a must-read for anyone in the financial services business.

I have known and worked with Vince for over thirty years, and when we were together at MetLife, he pioneered MetLife's dominance in multicultural markets. These are growing markets with great families and work ethics—the top ten cities in the US are now in a multicultural majority. If your organization doesn't reflect your community, you may not only be risking opportunity but your organization's very existence.

—**JOE JORDAN**, former VP of Insurance,
Paine Webber, and SVP at MetLife

Vince has been the voice in the insurance industry with the knowledge, passion, and expertise to grow distribution in multicultural markets.

—**GEORGE TSUI**, former President of the
Chinese American Insurance Association

DIVERSITY MEANS DOLLARS

7 SIMPLE STEPS TO CAPITALIZE ON THE CHANGING MARKETPLACE

VINCE VITIELLO

LIONCREST
PUBLISHING

DIVERSITY MEANS DOLLARS
7 Simple Steps to Capitalize on the Changing Marketplace

ISBN   978-1-5445-3924-9   *Hardcover*
      978-1-5445-3923-2   *Paperback*
      978-1-5445-3922-5   *Ebook*

To Janet, my wife, partner, and best friend, for
her continuous love and support

To my sons, Matthew and JonPeter, who
taught me about unconditional love

To my parents, who taught me how to reach for the stars

To my colleagues at New America Marketing
(NAM), for their dedication

Special thanks to those who have touched my life and career,
especially Chuck Kavitsky, who has had a great influence

CONTENTS

INTRODUCTION The Changing Face of America **1**

CHAPTER 1 Exponential Growth **17**

CHAPTER 2 Meeting the New Face of America **49**

CHAPTER 3 *Step One:* Selecting Your Market **65**

CHAPTER 4 *Step Two:* Market Immersion **79**

CHAPTER 5 *Step Three:* Building Your Unique Value Proposition **99**

CHAPTER 6 *Step Four:* Dollars In = 10X Growth **113**

CHAPTER 7 *Step Five:* Building Your Strategic Plan **131**

CHAPTER 8 *Step Six:* Market Ready—Tracking Your Progress **141**

CHAPTER 9 *Step Seven:* Doing Well by Doing Good **153**

CHAPTER 10 Selecting Your Next Market **165**

CONCLUSION The Changing Business of America **171**

About the Author **179**

THE CHANGING FACE OF AMERICA

"The diversity of America is a strength of the country, and I don't think that we use that."
—STEVE STOUTE

Imagine if some federal law mandated that you could only market to 30 percent of your potential customers. For the other 70 percent, you were not allowed to address them directly, speak their language, or refer to issues that matter most to them. You couldn't get to know them, learn about their culture, or become a presence in their communities.

It would be pretty ridiculous, wouldn't it? Of course, no such law exists. Nevertheless, in the largest American cities, where many businesses derive a large percentage of their overall revenue, business leaders market their products and services as if such laws were firmly in place. While the ten largest cities in the United States have populations that are 70 percent multicultural, many companies continue to use a one-size-fits-all approach to marketing.

The face of America is changing. It no longer looks like the primarily Caucasian world that most of us grew up in. While the United States has always been a nation of immigrants composed of diverse groups from many places, the growing pace of ethnic and racial diversity has accelerated in recent years in an incredible way.

This probably isn't news to you. Most of us experience this growing diversity in our daily lives. Just last week, I had a presentation in Philadelphia. I took an Uber to the airport, and my driver was a young Muslim man from Pakistan. At the airport, I went to Starbucks for a coffee, and the barista was Asian-American with an LGBTQ pride flag pinned to her apron. As I approached the gate for my flight, I passed an airport security guard who was African-American. And then I handed my ticket to the ticket handler, a Hispanic woman. Finally, I boarded my plane and greeted the pilot, an older gentleman from the Caribbean.

All along the way, I encountered and interacted with people from a diverse range of ethnic, racial, and social groups, and this wasn't a rare or unusual experience. If you live in any major city in the United States, you interact with diverse groups every day just going about your business. Even residents in smaller cities across the country are experiencing the daily reality of growing diversity.

But this sense of growing diversity isn't merely anecdotal. Data from the 2020 Census revealed that nearly four in ten Americans now identify as a race or ethnic group other than White. In fact, 2010 to 2020 was the first decade in the nation's history that saw a decline in the number of people who identify as White.[1] That

---

1   US Census Bureau. 2021. "2020 U.S. Population More Racially and Ethnically Diverse than Measured in 2010." The United States Census Bureau. August 12, 2021. https://www.census.gov/library/stories/2021/...

means racial and ethnic minorities accounted for *all* of the nation's population growth during that time.

Consider this: in 1980, White residents made up 80 percent of the population of the United States. By 2019, the White population had declined to 60.1 percent. And this decline in the White population has occurred in all fifty states.

These are just a few statistics out of many that reveal the growing diversity of America (we'll look at more later), and it's not just ethnic or racial diversity that's growing. The percentage of US adults who self-identify as lesbian, gay, bisexual, or transgender has increased to a new high of 7.1 percent, which is a 100 percent increase from 2012, when Gallup first measured it.[2]

But we're not simply talking about a numerical increase—the buying power of diverse groups has increased dramatically as well. From 1990 to 2021, the buying power of African-Americans, Asian-Americans,

...08/2020-united-states-population-more-racially-ethnically-diverse-than-2010.html.

2   Jones, Jeffrey. 2022. "LGBT Identification in U.S. Ticks up to 7.1%." Gallup. com. February 17, 2022. https://news.gallup.com/poll/389792/lgbt-identification-ticks-up.aspx.

and Hispanic-Americans grew tremendously. According to the University of Georgia's Selig Center for Economic Growth, these diverse groups now wield formidable economic clout.

"The Selig Center estimates the buying power for African-American, Asian-American, and Native American consumers, which has exploded over the past 30 years, up from $458 billion in 1990 to $3 trillion in 2020...Hispanic buying power also has grown substantially over the last 30 years, from $213 billion in 1990 to $1.9 trillion in 2020. Hispanic buying power accounted for 11.1% of US buying power in 2020, up from only 5% in 1990."

Furthermore, Asians are projected to be the largest immigrant group by 2050.

So, what does this mean for the business world?

REACHING DIVERSE MARKETS

The fact is, Millennials (those born 1981 to 1996) and Gen-Z (those born 1997 to 2012) are now the major consumers in all industries, and they are also the most diverse generations in history. No business can rely on the same old one-size-fits-all approach to marketing. If you fail to acknowledge this growing diversity, not only will you appear to be out of step with most of your consumers, but more than that, you will miss out on the exponential revenue opportunities in these diverse markets.

Understandably, trying to reach all of these diverse markets probably seems overwhelming. How in the world can you possibly craft targeted messaging to so many distinct ethnic, racial, and social groups? Well, here's the good news: you don't have to. In fact, the most effective approach is to identify *one* key market segment, get deep into that segment, and develop a strategy for marketing to them.

Many of these diverse market segments are underserved, so reaching out to them in a way that resonates strongly with who they are presents a huge opportunity to grow your top- and bottom-line revenue. In this book, I'm going to show you a seven-step process for doing just that.

We'll look more deeply at the changing face of America and discuss how you can identify some of these underserved market segments and select just one. Then we'll reveal a process for getting deep into your chosen market, building a value proposition to attract them, and gauging your investment in the market. We'll discuss how you can develop your marketing and measure your success.

Finally, once you've had success reaching an underserved market, we'll look at how you can choose the next one. After all, the opportunity is vast, and there are numerous market segments waiting for you to reach out to them with a message that resonates strongly. In the end, you will have the know-how to build a strategic plan for reaching a diverse market, execute it well, and then move on to the next market.

But why, you might ask, am I so passionate about reaching out to underserved diverse markets? Why does this matter to me? Allow me to explain by sharing a little bit about my background.

My name is Vince Vitiello, and I've served as chief marketing and distribution officer for a number of major financial services firms, including MetLife, Allianz of America, and National Life Group. I have more than thirty years of global experience working in diverse markets, both nationally and internationally, but my passion for diversity goes back much further than that.

You see, my father was an insurance agent. He was also bilingual—fluent in both English and Italian. In those days, insurance agents went house to house selling insurance policies, and individual agents were typically assigned a specific geographical area to service. Since he could speak the language and knew the culture, my father was assigned to an Italian-American community, and from an early age, I saw how he was able to connect deeply with his clients. His clients, most unfamiliar with financial nuances, relied on him for advice and counsel. His clients became our extended family.

The area where I grew up in New York City was mostly populated by Italians and people of Western European descent at that time. Since then, the population has shifted and is now comprised largely of Asian-Americans and Orthodox Jews. But the premise remains the same. These cultures want to be a part of the great American patchwork. They want to be served, but they have special needs, both in terms of language and culture.

When I worked for MetLife, I was responsible for growing sales and distribution across the entire right-hand side of the United States. Learning from my father's experiences, I looked for underserved diverse markets that needed our products and services. I saw tremendous opportunity in the Chinese community in the Northeast, so I dedicated significant resources to recruiting and training Chinese-American advisors.

Within ten years, MetLife had forty agencies run by Chinese leaders that accounted for 39 percent of the company's overall business. MetLife became the dominant player in the Chinese market because they focused on becoming part of the community. We dedicated resources to the initiative and stuck with it for years.

When I worked for Allianz, a global leader in insurance, I often visited their headquarters in Munich in 2002. Recently, I returned to Munich, and I was amazed at the changing demographics in the city. I spent a few days just watching people in cafes, restaurants, and shopping centers, and everywhere, the city has become far more diverse. In fact, almost 30 percent of Munich is now comprised of people who are foreign-born or have non-German roots.[3]

The leaders at Allianz saw this coming years earlier, thanks to the vision of former CEO Michael Diekmann, who is now a member of the company's advisory board. As a result, Allianz was at an advantage over many of their competitors when immigration accelerated in major cities around the world.

These demographic changes present opportunities for growth, but any business that intends to reach out to them in a meaningful way must market to them in a way that shows a deep understanding of *who they are*. It's a lesson I saw clearly in my father's experience, which was reinforced by my own experience, and it's more imperative than ever for leaders of organizations in all industries to embrace this approach.

---

3 Welle (www.dw.com), Deutsche. n.d. "Germany: Over 1 in 4 People Have 'Migrant Background' | DW | 12.04.2022." DW.COM. https://www.dw.com/en/germany-over-1-in-4-people-have-migrant-background/a-61452241.

Unfortunately, many companies are missing out on these opportunities without realizing it, and a big reason why they don't realize it is because their leadership doesn't reflect the diversity of the country. As I mentioned, I spent the bulk of my career in the financial services industry, specifically the life insurance business, working with many well-known insurance companies.

Many of the companies in this industry fully embraced diversity when immigration was robust in the early decades of the twentieth century. They employed hundreds of thousands of Irish, Italian, and Jewish immigrants as agents to sell to their own markets. As a result, they experienced exponential growth. For some reason, these same companies have been the slowest to realize the changing face of America in recent decades.

I recently attended a national leadership conference for the insurance industry. Of the 200 people who came to the conference, I saw not a single Asian-American, African-American, or Hispanic-American attendee. I spoke to some of the waiters and help staff, and they commented that they were the only people of color in the entire room.

This problem isn't limited to the insurance industry. It tends to be true in all older, historical industries. Companies are incredibly slow to realize just how much diverse leadership can transform their business and open them up to diverse markets. Their leadership continues to be "male, pale, and stale."

I have more than 15,000 contacts on LinkedIn and Instagram, and I routinely see business leaders posting pictures of their subordinates and up-and-coming new leaders; I think, *Where are the new faces of America? Why are the leaders of these businesses not as diverse as the country they operate in?* It's a huge missed opportunity for growth.

DOING WELL BY DOING GOOD

Of course, diversity affects the business world in many ways, both internally and externally. Before we go any further, let's take a moment to break down the various components of diversity. My good friends Janet and

Gary Smith lead the preeminent diversity firm called Ivy Planning Group. Among their clients are a number of Fortune 100 companies and even the US government. At various times in my role as a corporate leader, I have engaged them to assist my organization in becoming more diverse through *diversity*, *equity*, and *inclusion* (DEI) initiatives.

Janet and Gary Smith describe diversity in three separate segments: *workplace*, *workforce*, and *marketplace*. Ivy Planning Group is known for developing business strategies that integrate workforce, workplace, and marketplace diversity into a unified actionable plan. However, my focus in this book is entirely on the third pillar: generating revenue from diverse markets. This distinction is important because plenty of companies view diversity as a "check the box" necessity in hiring. But I'm here to show you how to generate revenue by reaching out to diverse markets.

Most companies are trying to figure out how to build an internal diversity culture, and there are plenty of books and resources to show you how to do that. Internal and external diversity go hand-in-hand in many ways, but our focus is on showing you how to produce revenue and do well for your company by doing good for these growing communities.

By marketing your products and services to a diverse market, you can help that community gain access to things they need or want but haven't had access to. Not only will you achieve exponential growth through these diverse markets, but you will begin serving them in a meaningful way. That's what I mean when I say *doing well by doing good.*

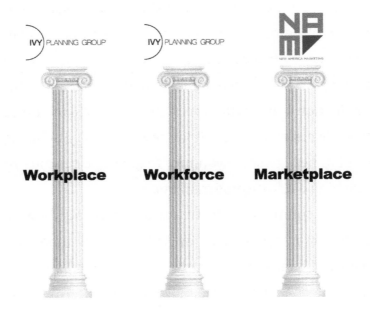

If you're ready for exponential growth, these markets are ready to do business with you! You can tap into the potential through seven simple steps:

1. Researching and selecting just one diverse market.
2. Immersing yourself in that market.
3. Building your unique value proposition for that market.
4. Investing in reaching that market.
5. Building a strategic marketing plan.
6. Tracking your progress.
7. Doing well by doing good.

This book will go step-by-step and guide you through how to leverage diversity for dollars. Let's get started by exploring the challenges of traditional growth and see how diverse marketing makes all the difference.

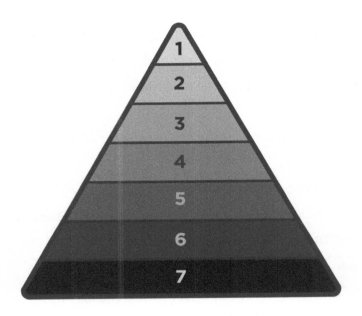

1. Researching and selecting just one diverse market.

2. Immersing yourself in that market.

3. Building your unique value proposition for that market.

4. Investing in reaching that market.

5. Building a strategic marketing plan.

6. Tracking your progress.

7. Doing well by doing good.

CHAPTER 1

EXPONENTIAL GROWTH

"Inclusion is not a matter of political correctness. It is the key to growth."

—REV. JESSE JACKSON

In 2021, corporate profit in the United States grew by a *dazzling* 3.4 percent across all industries.[4] That's hardly anything to get excited about. Compare this modest across-the-board increase to the more impressive

---

4   "United States Corporate Profits." 2019. Tradingeconomics.com. TRADING ECONOMICS. August 4, 2019. https://tradingeconomics.com/united-states/corporate-profits.

growth of specific companies. During that same year, Apple's profit increased by 28 percent, Microsoft by 50 percent, Meta by 20 percent, Tesla by 58 percent, and Alphabet experienced a staggering 65 percent growth in profit.

To what can we attribute this extreme difference in growth for certain companies? How have they managed to achieve such tremendous growth while the rest of the corporate world was practically at a standstill? I believe the answer may be found in the marketing strategies of these companies.

All of the high-growth companies I listed have strong diversity practices in their marketing. For example, Apple uses people from diverse groups almost exclusively in their advertisements. This is not merely coincidental. Apple's leaders have recognized the changing face of America, and they are reacting accordingly by crafting their messaging to appeal to previously underserved groups.

Today, even though 60 percent of Americans identify as non-White, more than 70 percent of business owners are White. Since most owners aren't part of these diverse groups, they might not be fully aware of the opportunities presented by changing demographics. Many of these diverse markets remain untapped, so the potential for exponential growth is unrealized. Even so, the majority of American companies appear to be clueless about this fact.

ONE SIZE DOESN'T FIT ALL

When tapping into diverse markets, you need to be culturally attuned to what is appropriate. We've all seen far too many examples of companies getting this wrong. In 2021, Walmart drew heat for selling a Juneteenth-themed ice cream flavor. While this may seem like an innocuous attempt to market to a minority group from the outside, it highlighted the fact that the company didn't understand the culture well enough to get the messaging right.

As a report from NBC explained, the product was "covered with images of the African continent and the colors—red, black, and green—long associated with the Black Liberation Movement in the US." However,

"Juneteenth is not a Pan-African holiday....the colors of the Juneteenth flag are red, white and blue on purpose. It is meant to signify the belonging of Black Americans in the fabric of the U.S."[5]

This is something that might not be obvious to individuals who are not familiar with African-American culture or history. Clearly, Walmart's leadership failed to do their research, and a well-meaning gesture landed flat.

Sometimes, a failed outreach to a diverse market is simply the result of not knowing the language well enough. In 2007, Visa created an ad campaign that was intended to reach the Spanish-speaking community in the US, and they used the slogan "La Vida Toma Visa." A literal translation of this phrase would be, "Life Takes Visa," but if you really know Spanish, then you understand that while the verb "tomar" technically means "to take," it's actually used most often to mean "to drink."

---

5   "Opinion | the Question We Have to Start Asking after Walmart's Juneteenth Mess." n.d. NBC News. https://www.nbcnews.com/think/opinion/walmarts-juneteenth-ice-cream-lack-understanding-black-experiences-rcna30888.

Therefore, the Spanish-speaking community read the Visa slogan as "Life Drinks Visa." It was confusing and made the company look culturally ignorant.[6]

Some companies simply don't do their due diligence and immerse themselves in a community before they attempt to market to them, so their attempts at multicultural branding come across as inauthentic and sometimes ignorant. Bad marketing ideas get approved in all-White boardrooms that are blatantly pandering to diverse markets, and they produce a negative response from the target audience. They may even wind up offending their target audience.

Dolce & Gabbana famously (or infamously) provoked outrage among the Asian (especially Chinese) community in 2018 when they attempted to reach out to that market with an ad campaign. The video advertisement showed a well-dressed Asian woman attempting to eat a pizza with chopsticks as Chinese folk music played

---

6   Boykiv, Yuriy. 2015. "Lessons from History's Worst Multicultural Marketing Campaigns." Inc.com. June 15, 2015. https://www.inc.com/yuriy-boykiv/lessons-from-history-s-worst-multicultural-marketing-campaigns.html.

in the background. The ad faced enormous backlash from Asian communities, who felt it was offensive and showed their culture as unintelligent. While the company's leaders eventually attempted to apologize in various ways, their apologies were not well received.

In 2017, at the height of the Black Lives Matter movement, when protests were taking place across the country over police brutality against African-Americans, Pepsi released an ad about the protests. In the ad, reality TV star Kendall Kenner is seen at a photoshoot when a protest march passes by. Jenner heads toward the march and sees a line of White police officers standing in the way. She approaches the officers and hands one of them a can of Pepsi. The officer takes a drink from the can, and the crowd of protesters cheers.

The can of Pepsi minimized the importance of the protests, and the backlash over this tone-deaf ad was swift and fierce. Pepsi was forced to end the campaign within one day and release a statement of apology to the public and to Kendall Jenner. As it turns out, the six people responsible for creating the ad were all

White.[7] Why didn't Pepsi hire people from the African-American community to provide them with a diverse perspective? We simply don't know, but it's probably because management had not spent the time to embrace the changing face of America and lacked the know-how to market to this diverse segment.

One of the more pointed criticisms of the ad came from Bernice King, daughter of Dr. Martin Luther King, Jr., who tweeted a picture of her father being shoved by a police officer with the caption, "If only Daddy would have known about the power of #Pepsi."

Speaking of Black Lives Matter, it was a very worthy cause, and it was interesting to see so many companies immediately rise up and contribute in some way. But how many companies did it as part of a sincere strategy to reach out to the African-American community, and how many of them simply did it as a kneejerk reaction in order to sound politically correct?

---

7   Rahman, Abid. 2017. Review of *Kendall Jenner Pepsi Commercial: How the "Worst Ad Ever" Came to Be.* Yahoo! Entertainment. April 6, 2017. https://www.yahoo.com/entertainment/kendall-jenner-pepsi-commercial-worst-ad-ever-came-102105777.html

Here we are a few years later, and what has the follow-up been? Have there been ongoing programs instituted? Why is it no longer on the front burner for many of the companies who were so vocal about it a few years ago?

In the 1970s, Mcdonald's attempted to reach out to the African-American community with a well-intentioned, but poorly received, ad that included the phrase, "Do Your Dinnertimin' at McDonald's." Another ad in the same campaign had the slogan, "Get Down with a Cheeseburger at McDonald's," that included a whole paragraph written in stereotypical "jive talk." It was a poorly researched attempt to "speak the language" of their target audience, and the tone came across as offensive and mocking. The ad campaign was a PR disaster for the company.

Of course, the McDonald's corporation now has an entire business unit dedicated to DEI, which is led by senior executives. Their robust DEI strategy influences the entire organization, including the home office, franchises, suppliers, and partnerships, and even their executive compensation is tied to DEI metrics. They have a supply chain of over 14 billion, so their supplier diversity program makes a huge impact. Twenty-three percent of suppliers are now diverse-owned, and suppliers sign a mutual commitment to diversity and inclusion, with actionable commitments to change within their own organizations.

They've certainly come a long way since their misguided ad campaign in the 1970s. And there are plenty of other examples of companies that have done diverse marketing well. In the 1990s, before the LGBTQ community had widespread public support, Subaru effectively marketed to lesbians. It was the time of "Don't Ask, Don't Tell" and the Defense of Marriage Act. Ellen DeGeneres hadn't yet revealed her sexual identity, and *Will and Grace* wasn't on the air. An IKEA ad in 1994 featuring a gay couple had led to a bomb threat, so targeting any part of the LGBTQ community was revolutionary and risky.

However, Subaru had learned in their market research that lesbians were four times more likely to buy a Subaru than the general public due to their love of dependability, the size of the vehicle, and even the name. At a time when most of the automobile industry was targeting eighteen-to-thirty-five-year-old White suburbanites, Subaru decided to target their most loyal niche.

However, because the broader culture was still not accepting of the LGBTQ community, they did so in a subtle way, using coded language and symbolism that lesbian consumers would understand even if they passed over the heads of the general public.

An ad might feature a car with a license plate that said, "Camp Out," or have a rainbow sticker on the bumper. Some ads featured the slogan, "It's not a choice. It's the way we're built." The company also supported LGBTQ causes. The community got the message, and the ad campaign proved to be very effective.

Rémy Martin also succeeded at reaching a diverse market. In fact, their success at reaching Chinese consumers provides a strong counterpoint to the failure of D&G's "chopstick pizza" ad. A carefully crafted Rémy Martin ad campaign in 2022 featured the beloved Chinese actor, singer, and brand ambassador Li Yifeng. Free of any negative cultural stereotypes, the ads show

Li "at a chic art exhibit, hugging friends, engaging in thoughtful conversation all while sipping on a glass of Rémy Martin Cognac."[8]

Li says, "Time is precious, so we should make sure we're spending it on only the best. Living our best years now, rather than waiting for them." Rémy Martin's careful marketing to Chinese consumers resulted in 40 percent of the sales for their XO liquor (a fine cognac) now coming from the Chinese market in the US.

What does this tell us? First of all, you have to understand the target market well enough that you won't inadvertently offend people. But it's also important to realize that you can't simply take your current marketing strategy and apply it to other diverse markets.

Historically, American businesses have been run by White male businessmen who have mostly marketed to other White males. Perhaps this marketing approach made economic sense (if not ethical or moral sense) in the past. However, in my years of

---

8   Howe, Nora. 2022. "Rémy Martin Toasts to the Good Life with New XO Campaign." Luxury Daily. January 25, 2022. https://www.luxurydaily.com/remy-martin-chinese-new-year-xo-campaign/.

consulting, I've been amazed at how many CEOs and CMOs are *still* completely unaware that the cities they do the majority of their business in are no longer predominantly White. They're not inadvertently offending diverse markets; rather, they're *not even trying to reach them*. The one-size-fits-all marketing approach is just not good enough.

THE EMPTY BUCKET

To be clear, I didn't share all of those ad campaign blunders in order to scare you. While it's true that the wrong approach can be worse than no approach, my purpose in writing this book isn't to discourage you or scare you away from marketing to diverse markets. To help you avoid any unintentional diversity blunders, I'm going to give a seven-simple-step approach for developing a robust, well-defined, and focused approach to diverse marketing in the next few chapters.

I spend much of my time now passionately trying to educate leaders on how diverse America has become and then convince them how much opportunity exists.

When I give a presentation, I always start by providing the demographic statistics, and I almost always see sober expressions followed by keen interest.

First, they can't believe it; for many, the extent of the changing face of America is a genuine surprise. They hadn't stopped to really think about it in depth.

Second, they realize just how much untapped marketing potential is out there, and they are astonished and hopeful. Some of these business leaders have been struggling to grow their businesses for years, and once the blinders are taken off, they discover many opportunities for growth right around them.

That's not to say that US business leaders are completely blind to the growing need for diversity, but their gaze is largely turned inward. You might think you are already embracing diversity because you have implemented some internal changes, but that doesn't mean you have fully realized the external potential of marketing to diverse groups.

As diversity in America grows, businesses must adapt to meet the demands of the new marketplace. It's no longer acceptable to continue marketing, largely or exclusively, to older White men. Indeed, it may actually be harmful to your brand, because growing diverse markets will see it and say, "This product clearly isn't meant for me."

Research shows that 70 percent of consumers are more likely to choose one brand over another if that brand demonstrates inclusion and diversity in its promotions and offers.[9] Additionally, more inclusive ads increase the purchase intent of younger consumers by 23 percent. Also, 61 percent of all Americans find diversity in advertising important.

People today expect to see diversity in marketing, and most consumers will hold it against a company if they don't. In other words, reaching out to diverse markets not only attracts that market, but it also attracts those outside of the market who *expect it*. And why do they expect it? Because they feel that it is the right thing to do. So there is a moral and ethical element to reaching out to diverse markets. It's not merely a

9   "By the Numbers: Diversity and Inclusion Are Good for Business." Detroit Regional Chamber. April 21, 2022. https://www.detroitchamber.com/by-the-numbers-diversity-and-inclusion-are-good-for-business/.

money-making opportunity, but an effort to include ethnic, racial, and social groups who have been historically underserved.

Coca-Cola started using diverse people in their advertisements way back in 1955, when they created an ad campaign that featured Mary Alexander, an African-American woman.[10] They did it not just to capitalize on a diversifying population of consumers, but also as a way to embrace the change in society and give marginalized people a voice. In that sense, embracing diversity in your marketing is both 1) a smart business move in response to your changing customer base and 2) the right thing to do.

Many organizations begin their journey into diverse marketing by taking what they feel is the easiest step: translating all of their marketing collateral into the language of their chosen market. While it's a worthy first step, without a sound marketing plan around it,

---

10 "Mary Alexander, the First African American Woman in Coke Ads - News & Articles." 2013. Coca-Colacompany.com. 2013. https://www. coca-colacompany.com/news/mary-alexander-the-first-african-american-woman-in-coke-ads.

the collateral is never going to get into the hands of the right potential customers.

When you create a website for your business, you have to drive traffic to that website in order to get business. Similarly, just because you create a detailed, fully functional website in the language of your target audience doesn't mean you're going to automatically get business unless you drive traffic to the website. In the end, it might wind up being a useless, costly investment. Similarly, translating brochures without getting them into the hands of your target audience will only become a frustrating experience, and it might lead you to abandon your efforts in diverse marketing.

An easy first step can't take the place of a detailed marketing plan, so don't jump for the lowest-hanging fruit in each chapter. Attack the market with a professionally, well-thought-out marketing plan.

"DON'T I ALREADY DO THAT?"

When I speak on this subject, there's a response that I get quite often. It usually takes the form of a rebuttal that goes something like this: "I already have diverse customers, so why do I need to change? And if I have diverse customers, doesn't that mean I'm already doing what I need to do to reach them?"

Their mistake is confusing a *conscious strategy* with a *subconscious competency*. The latter cannot take the place of the former, because unless you are intentional about reaching diverse markets, you will never realize the full growth potential they offer. Therefore, they need to trade their, "I'm already doing it" mentality with a mindset that asks, "How can I dominate diverse markets? How can I capitalize on the new marketplace?"

Rémy Martin already had Chinese consumers when they started putting strategy behind their diverse marketing. They didn't shrug and say, "Well, we already have some Chinese customers, so why should we spend money creating ads that target them?" Instead, they expertly marketed their products in a way that showed an understanding and empathy for the Chinese market, and as a result, they are now a dominant liquor company in that market.

So, even if you have some diverse customers, it doesn't mean you don't need to strategize further. How are you going to truly embrace diverse markets in order to dominate the competition? Let's look at how you can start to do just that.

WHERE TO START

Where does any business initiative start? At the top— with the CEO.

In my years of consulting, it has become crystal clear that the single common denominator in every business transformation—especially diverse marketing—starts with the CEO creating and clearly communicating a vision. This usually comes about in one of three ways.

Sometimes, the CEO sees the incredible opportunity available and wants to implement steps to capitalize on their diverse clientele. Other times, the CEO is simply reacting to a potential problem, trying to "nip it in the bud." They may think, "Well, we'd better start reaching out to diverse markets before we fall behind the competition." Finally, and unfortunately, I'm sometimes called in to assist companies in making the change because they're facing a lawsuit or negative publicity, but, as I say, better late than never.

Regardless of the impetus, once the CEO and leadership are on board to create change, it doesn't take long for them to realize just how much opportunity is available in diverse markets.

When I was at MetLife, I distinctly recall the time our CEO decided to make this switch. He called a meeting for all of our senior executives. We took our seats in the conference room and waited. Finally, he strode into the room and approached the podium. He gestured at the people gathered in the room.

"We don't look like our marketplace," he said. "I'm going to change that."

He was a true visionary because he saw what the market was like, and he had the resolve to make the necessary changes in order to reach it. Though it took some hard work, in the end, embracing diverse markets paid off for MetLife in a major way. Our performance regarding diversity was tied to metrics and compensation. Our approach to these markets was not begun as a charity or "do the right thing,"—it was developed as a business strategy to drive revenue.

A diversity opportunity initiative is rarely easy. To pull it off, you need a strong advocate in your company who is willing to keep moving it forward. A member (or some members) of the highest level of your organization must be a visionary who will constantly push for change. This is no small feat, but it will change your business to its core. Every team member will be affected in some way, and they're going to want a compelling reason *why*.

If you have a board of directors, be sure to include them at the start of your diversity journey. In my experience, most boards of directors are still dominated by seasoned Caucasian board members with, perhaps, one or two newer diverse members. However, when I present the idea of diverse marketing, they always respond favorably for two reasons.

First, it's the right thing to do. Second, they see it as a revenue opportunity. There may be a few doubters among the old-line board members, who feel like they are being pushed into political correctness, but they rarely express these concerns openly. Start with your board, sharing the demographic opportunity for your product or service, and then conduct subsequent meetings with a detailed marketing plan. Manage their expectations. Keep the board updated with good anecdotal stories of progress, and it will go a long way toward keeping your company on the right track. Manage their fears about costs. In addition, many will feel the need to totally reinvent the company and move away from the company's core. This is not a change of culture; costs and investments will be incremental. Remember, this is a journey and will take some time.

CHANGE FROM TOP TO BOTTOM

Bear in mind, when you decide to include diversity in your marketing efforts, it's going to affect your overall business strategy. Consider how different your company would look if 40 percent of your business was coming from diverse markets. How would your messaging change? What would your marketing emails look like? Who would you reach out to for affiliate marketing? Who would you hire to get closer to your selected market?

You will have to think through many questions like these. Whatever you do, make sure your decisions about marketing and messaging are driven by data and are culturally attuned to your target market. You don't want to expend a lot of time, effort, and resources just to create the next "chopstick pizza" fiasco.

When developing a diverse marketing strategy, it's important first of all to understand what percentage of your existing business already comes from diverse groups. That doesn't necessarily mean that you should go out and start asking people their ethnicity. In fact, that might be poorly received and drive some people away.

Some of the companies I worked with in the past hired outside firms to analyze our customer database. Using surnames, zip codes, and immigration data, these outside firms were able to identify consumer diversity, including country of origin, with 90 percent accuracy. It required an investment up front, but the data the companies received was invaluable and enabled us to create a baseline for further diversity efforts.

But here's the good news. This process can be done much more simply and at much less cost. Let's suppose you decide, like Rémy Martin, to reach out to the Chinese market. It might be overwhelming to think about the billion-plus Chinese people in the world. Your first step is to determine what percentage of your existing customer base is already part of this community. The easiest way to go about it is to conduct a simple Google search to determine the most common Chinese surnames.

As it turns out, there are a handful of surnames that are shared by most of the Chinese population. Actually, the five most common surnames in China (Wang, Li, Zhang, Liu, Chen) are shared by more than 433 million people in China.[11] The same is true for Chinese surnames here in America. Apply these surnames to your customer base, and you will quickly be able to

---

11 Jessie Yeung. n.d. "How Rare Names Go Extinct in China's Modern Digital Age." CNN. Accessed September 11, 2022. https://www.cnn.com/2021/01/16/china/chinese-names-few-intl-hnk-dst/index.html.

determine roughly how many of your current customers are Chinese with a reasonable degree of accuracy. The same process can be used with other diverse groups as well. Be sure to consult with your legal department for advice and counsel for how to go about utilizing surnames within your customer database.

Knowing the percentage of your current customer base from the Chinese segment reveals how successful you already are at reaching this diverse market. Next, you need to determine and allocate the resources, both financial and human, that will be devoted to an increased focus on marketing to that group. Just remember, penetrating a specific market and monitoring the results will take time, effort, and money.

Again, it helps to have a visionary leader who can carry your company through this process. Finally, create a baseline of where you are today and set a clear goal for where you hope to be with your diverse marketing initiative in a few years. That way, you can set milestones and track your progress, which will provide ongoing encouragement to your teams. This is the essence of the process that we're going to discuss in the following chapters, but before you can implement the process, you have to overcome any resistance, doubts, or excuses.

As you begin your journey, not everyone on your team or among your current customer base will be on board with your plan. I once made a presentation on diverse marketing to the CEO and executive team of a major retailer that sold basic American fashion. Their target customers were typical Ivy League, country-club types.

I anticipated that they might have some doubts about their need for diverse marketing, so as part of my presentation, I first showed them a picture of the 1965 Princeton graduating class. There were about a hundred students and all of them were White men. Then I showed them a picture of the 2019 Princeton graduating class, and it was an incredibly diverse group, both in terms of gender and ethnicity.

"The Ivy League doesn't look or dress the same way anymore," I said.

Even so, the design team still pushed back. They wanted to protect their brand and the reputation they'd built, so they resisted focusing on diverse marketing.

To make a long story short, the retailer went bankrupt during the pandemic. This is an example of a lack of diversity input.

On another occasion, I spoke with an insurance group that was interested in recruiting advisors in diverse markets, especially the Hispanic-, Asian-, and African-American communities. Geographically, they were focused on the Southeast United States, right in the heart of the Bible Belt, so they had no interest in including the LGBTQ community in their diverse marketing initiatives for religious reasons.

In my own firm, I always conducted marketing outreach and posted social media messages for special ethnic and religious holidays throughout the year. When the message was about a Jewish or Christian holiday, no one ever complained. But when we included Muslim holidays like Ramadan and Eid, we received some nasty comments from people.

This kind of pushback happens, but you can't let it stop you from doing what you know is right. Nevertheless, be ready to address and deal with it. Understand not everyone will be as open as you are.

THE TIMES, THEY ARE A-CHANGIN'

You're also going to encounter some excuses for why you can't do this. There's an excuse I often encounter when speaking to CEOs and business leaders about this transformation. They'll say something like, "But I'm not a member of a diverse group. How can I target a diverse market?"

It's this kind of thinking that contributes to the problem in the first place. If business leaders only reach out to people that look like themselves or target markets that they're already familiar with, then many growing markets are going to remain underserved. A whole lot of untapped potential will be unrealized, and indeed, these companies will find themselves falling further and further behind as the face of America continues to change.

Even in 2022, the typical CEO is a White male. He loves golf. He belongs to a mostly—or exclusively—White country club, and he lives in the suburbs. He mostly deals with other like-minded CEOs. Although he may visit major cities where the population is diverse, he's typically only there for a meeting or special dinner, and he's meeting with people from a similar background as himself.

Despite these facts, even the most non-diverse leader can lead the charge and succeed in diverse marketing as long as they're willing to study and become immersed in the diverse marketplace. In my experience, a White leader who is willing to do this becomes a rockstar to many of their employees from diverse backgrounds.

As I mentioned in the Introduction, my own family came here from Italy. I am Caucasian, so I don't belong to any of these growing diverse markets. Nevertheless, despite this fact, I have taken companies through the process of reaching out to diverse markets many times, and *it has been profitable every single time*. When done right, this kind of transformation is always a positive experience for the company and the new target market.

It doesn't matter if you are personally a member of a diverse group. I live in a Long Island suburb that is mostly White, but there's a local White-owned restaurant and dance club that has become a popular weekend meeting place for local and not-so-local Hispanic-Americans. Why? Because they advertise to the Hispanic-American community, and they've created a robust social media program to reach out to them. Their website is in Spanish, their menu contains plenty of Hispanic foods, and their music is performed by a Hispanic DJ.

Whatever your ethnic, racial, or social identity happens to be, you can still commit to creating change in your company by building and developing diverse markets that reflect the changes all around you. In the process, you will give more consumers a voice in your company, and these diverse markets will gain access to products and services that they might not have had access to before.

In other words, you have everything to gain and nothing to lose!

Accept first that America is changing. These changes aren't limited to race, but include sexual orientation, gender identification, socioeconomic status, political perspective, spirituality, age, and disability. This nation is more diverse than ever before *in more ways than ever before*. While all these groups desire to be part of the American fabric, providing them individualized attention can create dramatic revenue growth for your firm.

You should focus on meeting the change both internally and externally. As we said, diversity initiatives inside your company go hand-in-hand with a greater focus on diverse marketing. Too many companies focus on the former while continuing to neglect the latter, but there is a powerful synergy in combining the two.

Some companies are getting this right and reaping the rewards. They've recognized the change and adjusted accordingly; the younger generations of consumers are responding with greater enthusiasm. So what about your company? How much business do you already get from diverse groups? How much farther do you have to go to truly embrace diverse marketing? And how much potential remains unrealized because you haven't yet reached out to some key groups who would love your products and services if you only spoke to them in a way that resonated with their culture and community?

Too many times, the person leading the diversity initiative in a company asks his team how they feel about the initiative. This is a business initiative. It's not about feelings. It's similar to launching a new product on the company shelf. Push through the feelings; get the team to go out and sell diversity as a business initiative. Tie their performance to the success metrics of the program (as you would do for a new product launch) and to their compensation.

No matter where you're at currently, with proper planning and focus, you can add diversity to your overall business plan and begin to take hold of that coveted exponential growth.

CHAPTER 2

MEETING THE NEW FACE OF AMERICA

"It is not the strongest of the species that survives, nor the most intelligent. It is the one that is most adaptable to change."

—CHARLES DARWIN

New York, Los Angeles, Chicago, Philadelphia, Dallas, Houston, San Antonio, San Diego, Phoenix, and San Jose—these are the ten largest cities in the United States of America today. If you do any business at all across the nation, then you probably have some vested interest in these cities. However, if you're like many companies, you might not realize that the populations of these cities are now predominantly multicultural.

Since 1980, as you can see by this graph, the White population started at just under 80 percent. Fast forward forty years, and the White population has shrunk to 57.8 percent. Conversely, the Hispanic population has grown from 6.4 percent to 18.7 percent. The Black population has remained roughly the same, but the Asian population has gone from being negligible to 5.9 percent.

Sadly, I've seen many companies continue to market in these major cities the same way they did twenty or thirty years ago, oblivious to just how much things have changed. As we mentioned in the introduction, America's ever-increasing population is largely due to immigration and the astounding birth rates among diverse groups. This is where America is growing. One-size-fits-all marketing no longer works.

As a result of growing diverse groups coupled with longer life expectancy, the population of America has doubled over the past sixty years, from 160 million people in the 1960s to 330 million today.

Consider these Census facts: today, out of all Americans, 62 million are Hispanic-American, 41 million are African-American, and 20 million are Asian-American. Ethnic populations are easily verifiable. The LGBTQ population is estimated to be 20 million.[12] There are seven million Asian-American people living in California alone, and 25 percent of Florida is Hispanic-American. If the 12 million Texas Hispanic-Americans were their own state, they would be the fifth largest state in the US. In addition, for the first time in our nation's history, Census information has revealed that the population of Caucasians has gotten smaller by 9 percent. Do you happen to know who the fastest-growing diverse group in the United States is? The answer is: Hasidic Orthodox Jews, who average eight to ten children per family.

---

12 Brooke Migdon | Dec. 14, 2021. 2021. "US LGBTQ+ Population Hits 20 Million." The Hill. December 14, 2021. https://thehill.com/changing-america/respect/diversity-inclusion/585711-us-lgbtq-population-hits-20-million/.

But the ethnic and racial lines are occasionally blurry. For example, thirty-four million people consider themselves part of more than one race. Ten years ago, it was only nine million, and twenty years ago, it was only six million. That is true exponential growth.

If you're like most of my regular clients, at least some of these statistics will come as a shock to you. It turns out that America's demographics have changed without many people noticing the extent of it and, as a result, the impact on consumer buying. You might not have realized that the old days of generic White-focused marketing are gone. While you may still be committed to "business as usual," the nation has transformed around you.

You're not alone. Many business, especially small- to mid-sized businesses, are in the same boat. But with great change come great opportunity. This shift to a more diverse country had created some enormous markets that are still largely untapped by most businesses.

It's at this point when speaking to clients that their eyes start to light up, and their minds start racing. If you're not there yet, consider the following. Imagine you started catering to the growing Hispanic market in America. Suddenly, you would be opening yourself up to almost 20 percent of the country. What effect would that have on your business? Would it double your profits? Triple them? 10X them?

Enormous diverse markets are out there just waiting for you to recognize them, embrace them, and act on the opportunity!

WALK A MILE IN THEIR SHOES

The opportunity should be crystal clear, but let's put you in the shoes of some of these diverse markets by taking an imaginary trip. Statistically speaking, you are probably White, but if you're not, imagine for a moment that you are. As a Caucasian, English-speaking American, you find yourself being transferred to Beijing, China, for your job.

Upon arrival, you settle into your apartment, and now you have to figure out how to live life and meet your needs as a foreign resident in Beijing. First, you decide you need to purchase an automobile, something with good fuel economy for your daily commute to work, so how do you go about doing that? You start by going on the internet and finding a local dealer's website, but the website is only in Mandarin. And you've only just begun to learn the language.

This deters you from contacting the dealer through the internet, so you decide to use China's version of an 800 number. After dialing, however, you get hold of someone who doesn't speak English. Frustrated, you hang up and decide to walk to a nearby used car lot you saw on a billboard on the way to your apartment.

The bad luck continues. The salesman at the used car dealership only speaks broken English. He figures out that you want a car, but all of the forms are in Mandarin. He struggles to translate, and eventually, the deal falls apart. On the way back to your apartment, you consider all of the difficulties you're having.

You start to think, *I really don't fit in here. These people don't want to do business with me.*

If this were America, you'd probably already be driving your newly purchased car home by now. Instead, you're walking back home empty-handed, and you feel completely out of place in your new country. How in the world are you ever going to fit in? Learning the language is going to take you a long time. You know that. In fact, you might never become fully fluent in Mandarin. So how in the world are you supposed to get by?

Now you think, *I would gladly pay someone a premium price if they could help me with my vehicle purchase.*

And then a billboard catches your eye. It's an advertisement from another local dealer for a small coupe, exactly the kind of car you were hoping to buy. However, the thing that really draws your attention is a small phrase in the bottom corner of the billboard. In bold letters, it declares, "We speak English."

Imagine how grateful you would feel in that moment. How relieved, accepted, and *wanted.* Here's a car dealer who *wants* your business, and they're willing to go out of their way to speak your language and help you get what you need. In addition to speaking English, they are also able to educate you on how to finance in China, what the specific tax implications are, how to purchase auto insurance, how to register your car, how to apply for a Chinese driver's license, and driving tips for American citizens. In other words, in addition to language, this dealer has developed a unique value proposition that caters to American citizens and totally differentiates his dealership from others.

You're probably going to become a loyal customer of that dealer, and there's a good chance you'll continue buying cars from them when the need arises years into the future, even after you've become fluent in Mandarin. Additionally, when you talk to other American ex-pats living in Beijing, you're going to recommend that business. Imagine the additional revenue that this business would receive because of its awareness and sensitivity to this specific market.

"Hey, if you're in the market for a new car, I know a place that caters to American citizens, and all they need to know about owning, financing, and driving a car in China!"

Now, apply this story to an immigrant inquiring about your products or services. Imagine how readily they would flock to your business if you had a website with multiple language options, including their own, an 800 number that offered their native language, forms in their language, and perhaps even salespeople who understood their culture and addressed certain culturally-specific concerns. Do you suppose they would tell their friends, family, and other members of their community about your business? Of course, they would!

"Hey, friends, here is a company that *wants* our business! They speak our language, and they understand us. You have to check them out!"

What if, after buying from you and becoming a customer, that immigrant received a greeting card from your business on one of their native country's traditional holidays? How much more would they feel like you want their business and strive to understand them?

There's real power in this sort of messaging. Whether you celebrate Lunar New Year with your Chinese consumers or recognize Pride Month with the LGBTQ community, embracing diversity and differences is the name of the game when it comes to winning the business of diverse markets. And the deeper you dive into the culture, the more people in that group will begin to feel comfortable being associated with your company—and the more business you'll receive from them.

I'm very interested in the Hasidic community. While it's a relatively small segment of the market compared to African-Americans or Hispanic-Americans, it is nevertheless exploding in size. In fact, the Hasidic community is the fastest-growing diverse segment in this country, but it's largely unrecognized because it's a closed community.

If you don't happen to operate your business in Brooklyn, Upstate New York, or Central New Jersey, then they might never appear on your marketing radar. The reason why they are exploding in size is that the typical Hasidic family consists of eight to ten children, and the typical marriage occurs at age eighteen.

Think about when you were in fifth grade. How many different fifth-grade classrooms were there in your school? Probably just a few. But in the Brooklyn school of the Hasidic Jewish community, there are eighty-two fifth-grade classes, with boys and girls attending school in separate buildings. The same is true of every grade all the way through high school. There is huge untapped potential in the Hasidic community for businesses that are willing to get to know them and become immersed in the community.

Another example is if you pass a construction site nowadays, chances are many of the workers will be Hispanic. Most of them might not speak English, so who is servicing the construction market? Where are these workers buying their equipment? Where do they buy their lunches during break? Where do they buy their cars? Someone is going to cater to these construction workers and benefit from offering them the products and services they need and want. Landscaping companies are now predominantly employed by Hispanic people. In fact, many of these businesses are owned and operated by Hispanics.

DIVERSITY FOR THE COMMON PEOPLE

The subject of diversity almost certainly isn't new to you. Everyone is aware of at least some of the ongoing discussion about the growing diversity in America, but most people think about diversity almost exclusively in regard to political debates, PR debacles, and lawsuits.

The actual reality and impact of diverse markets in America remains largely unknown to many business leaders. They just don't realize the vast opportunities that are out there or how fast those opportunities are growing. It shouldn't be a complete surprise to you. If you live or work in a big city, then you come face-to-face with our growing diversity every day. Think about your day thus far. How many individuals from diverse markets did you see or interact with today just going about your business?

Even if you're located in a small city, chances are you've seen some indication of the growing diversity in this nation. For example, St. Paul, Minnesota, now contains the largest urban Hmong [Southwest Chinese, Vietnamese, Thailand, and others] population in the world. A business in St. Paul that embraces this community could explode in size. That's just one small example out of thousands. Indeed, the next time you go out to eat, shop, travel, or work, take a little time to look around you. Notice just how diverse the populace has become where you live. This isn't happening in some far away place. It's happening right where you are. And it's certainly *not* something to be afraid of.

A lot of what we've been talking about are major metropolitan areas as well as states like Florida, Texas, California, New York, and New Jersey. However, diversity is exploding not just in these larger states. As an example, Iowa would not be a considered a hotbed for diversity in middle America. However, 6 percent of the population there is Hispanic. The Hispanic-American population has grown 130 percent in the last thirty years. Politicians in Iowa are now paying attention to the shifting demographics. Twenty-five percent of Hispanics are in manufacturing, fifteen are in education, and 5,000 own small businesses. This Hispanic-American community communicates with each other. Many of them share the same houses of worship, are on similar social media outlets, and attend similar cultural events. So the point of entry in this group is relatively inexpensive and easy. Remember, if you do the right thing for the community, it's easy to get your message spread quickly. The opposite is also true.

Diversity brings opportunity. The exponential growth you've always dreamed about might be right at your fingertips. You have to tap into these growing markets. Diverse groups are not emerging markets—they're *exploding*. One Chinatown in New York City has become *nine* Chinatowns. Most people who have visited New York are familiar with the Manhattan Chinatown, but there are other exploding Chinatowns. The second biggest is in Flushing, which is adjacent to LaGuardia airport, and the third biggest is in Sunset Park, Brooklyn. There are six other areas that have become densely populated with Chinese immigrants, and over the next few years, these individual Chinatowns will become so large that they are close to becoming connected to each other. There are over 1 million Chinese residents in New York City. That is a clear indication of the exponential opportunity.

There are companies out there enjoying amazing growth by reaching out to these diverse markets. Will you be one of them? Someone is going to dominate them. Will it be you?

Now you might be thinking, *I want to implement more diversity in our marketing and messaging, but I don't even know where to begin.* You don't start by try-ing to reach *everyone*. You start by identifying just one diverse market and going after them. We'll look at how you begin to do that in the next chapter.

CHAPTER 3

STEP ONE: SELECTING YOUR MARKET

"Diversity of thought and culture
and religion and ideas has become
the strength of America."

—GARY LOCKE

By now, you should at least have a sense of the incredible opportunity that is yours for the taking. I've been trying to get you motivated and excited about the growth potential that you can find in diverse marketing, but now it's time for me to pull the reins a bit.

Once I reveal the sheer amount of business that's available with diverse marketing, many CEOs get so excited they immediately want to "boil the ocean." If that's how you feel right now, then I applaud your enthusiasm. That kind of enthusiasm will be needed. However, you can't rush out and immediately reach every diverse market in the country.

You have to start by selecting just one market, learning it inside and out, then becoming its dominant provider of your type of products or services, either locally or nationally.

THE US CENSUS

When selecting a market, it is imperative that your choice be data-driven, and there's no better source of data-driven information on demographics in this country than the US Census. The Census is actually mandated by Article I, Section 2 of the US Constitution, which directs "counting the whole number of persons in each State, excluding Indians not taxed," every ten years.

This process is carried about by the United States Census Bureau, which is part of the Department of Commerce. Since the results of the Census are used to allocate the seats in the US House of Representatives and informed decisions about the use of federal and state funds, a vast amount of time and resources is devoted to the effort. Many federal, state, local, and even tribal governments use Census data for making important decisions.

Besides the ten-year Census, the bureau also conducts an economic census every five years, a survey of state and local governments every five years, and an annual American Community Survey (ACS) that shows what the US population looks like and how it lives. Additionally, every year, the Bureau publishes population estimates and the demographic components of population changes, such as births, deaths, and migration.[13]

---

13 US Census Bureau. 2017. "U.S. Census Bureau at a Glance." The United States Census Bureau. October 24, 2017. https://www.census.gov/about/what/census-at-a-glance.html.

The information on the Census website is hands-down the greatest diversity marketing data you can find, and best of all, you can access the data for free at *census.gov*.

Let's suppose you and your team have decided to start making significant inroads into the Hispanic-American market. You'd like to create ten retail real estate offices that exclusively cater to the recent Hispanic immigrant homebuyer and broker. Because your team is domiciled throughout Texas and the Southwest, you have chosen to first move into a more familiar geographical area. So you narrow it down to two distinct markets: Houston or Phoenix. You advise your team not to "boil the ocean," but to select just one diverse segment in just one of these two geographical locations.

Your next best step is to go to *census.gov* and conduct some research about these two markets. When you navigate to the Census homepage, the first things you're going to see are the US and the world populations, which are updated daily. It will look something like this:

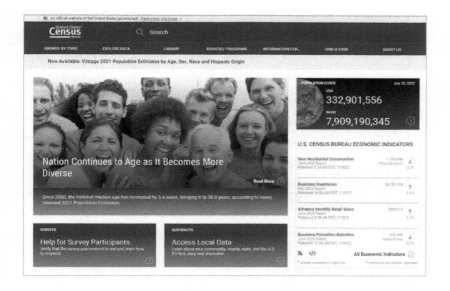

At the time of this writing, the homepage also included a link to a timely article about the nation becoming older and more diverse, but this will probably be different by the time you read this. You will also see a population clock, which is in real time and changes on a daily basis. Your next step is to click on the box that says "Access Local Data." This will take you to a page of quick facts that looks something like the graphic on the following page.

This and all census data was generated from the 2020 United States Census at *data.census.gov*.

POPULATION	UNITED STATES
Population estimates, July 1, 2021 - (V2021)	331,893,745
Population estimates base, April 1, 2020 - (V2021)	331,449,281
Population, percent change - April 1, 2020 (V2021) (estimates base) to July 1, 2021	0.1%
Population, Census, April 1, 2020	331,449,281
Population, Census, April 1, 2010	308,745,538
AGE AND SEX	--
Persons under 5 years, percent	5.7%
Persons under 18 years, percent	22.2%
Persons age 65 years and over, percent	16.8%
Female persons, percent	50.5%
RACE AND HISPANIC ORIGIN	--
White alone, percent	75.8%
Black or African American alone, percent	13.6%
American Indian and Alaska Native alone, percent	1.3%
Asian alone, percent	6.1%
Native Hawaiian and Other Pacific Islander alone, percent	0.3%
Two or more races, percent	2.9%
Hispanic or Latino, percent	18.9%
White alone, not Hispanic or Latino, percent	59.3%

You can enter a state, county, city, town, or zip code in the search bar at the top of the page to get data on specific geographical areas. So, first, you enter "Houston city" into this box, and the website provides you with localized data about that city. It also compares this local data to national numbers. As an example, you can see that the US population is at 331,893,745 (see the graphic on the following page).

As you can see, the city of Houston has a population of 2,288,250 people (as of the most recent Census, July 2021), compared to the national population of 331,893,745. According to the data, Houston is 44 percent Hispanic, with 28.9 percent being foreign-born, and 48.4 percent of the population of the city speaking a language other than English at home. As you scroll down the page, you also find that the mean travel time to work is 27.6 minutes, broadband usage is 83.9 percent, and the percentage of people who have a computer at home is 93.8 percent.

Now, you need to compare the data for Houston with the data for Phoenix so you can determine which of these markets will be a better first step for your company.

POPULATION	HOUSTON, TEXAS (CITY)	UNITED STATES
Population estimates, July 1, 2021 - (V2021)	⚠ 2,288,250	⚠ 331,893,745
Population estimates base, April 1, 2020 - (V2021)	⚠ 2,302,792	⚠ 331,449,281
Population, percent change - April 1, 2020 (V2021) (estimates base) to July 1, 2021	⚠ -0.6%	⚠ 0.1%
Population, Census, April 1, 2020	2,304,580	331,449,281
Population, Census, April 1, 2010	2,099,451	308,745,538
AGE AND SEX	--	--
Persons under 5 years, percent	⚠ 7.5%	⚠ 5.7%
Persons under 18 years, percent	⚠ 24.7%	⚠ 22.2%
Persons age 65 years and over, percent	⚠ 11.0%	⚠ 16.8%
Female persons, percent	⚠ 50.2%	⚠ 50.5%
RACE AND HISPANIC ORIGIN	--	--
White alone, percent	⚠ 51.5%	⚠ 75.8%
Black or African American alone, percent	⚠ 22.8%	⚠ 13.6%
American Indian and Alaska Native alone, percent	⚠ 0.3%	⚠ 1.3%
Asian alone, percent	⚠ 6.9%	⚠ 6.1%
Native Hawaiian and Other Pacific Islander alone, percent	⚠ 0.0%	⚠ 0.3%
Two or more races, percent	⚠ 7.0%	⚠ 2.9%
Hispanic or Latino, percent	⚠ 44.5%	⚠ 18.9%
White alone, not Hispanic or Latino, percent	⚠ 24.1%	⚠ 59.3%
POPULATION CHARACTERISTICS	--	--
Veterans, 2016-2020	69,023	17,835,456
Foreign-born persons, percent, 2016-2020	28.9%	13.5%
HOUSING	--	--
Housing units, July 1, 2021, (V2021)	X	142,153,010
Owner-occupied housing unit rate, 2016-2020	42.9%	64.4%
Median value of owner-occupied housing units, 2016-2020	$186,800	$229,800
Median selected monthly owner costs-with a mortgage, 2016-2020	$1,691	$1,621
Median selected monthly owner costs-without a mortgage, 2016-2020	$541	$509
Median gross rent, 2016-2020	$1,086	$1,096
Building permits, 2021	X	1,736,982
FAMILIES & LIVING ARRANGEMENTS	--	--
Households, 2016-2020	874,827	122,354,219
Persons per household, 2016-2020	2.61	2.60
Living in same house 1 year ago, percent of persons age 1+ year, 2016-2020	82.0%	86.2%
Language other than English spoken at home, percent of persons age 5+ years, 2016-2020	48.4%	21.5%
COMPUTER AND INTERNET USE	--	--
Households with a computer, percent, 2016-2020	91.5%	88.58%
Households with a broadband Internet subscription, percent, 2016-2020	34.3%	32.9%
EDUCATION	HOUSTON, TEXAS	UNITED STATES
High school graduate or higher, percent of persons age 25+ years, 2016-2020	79.7%	91.9%
Bachelor's degree or higher, percent of persons age 25+ years, 2016-2020	83.9%	85.2%
HEALTH	--	--
With a disability, under age 65 years, percent, 2016-2020	6.6%	8.7%
Persons without health insurance, under age 65 years, percent	⚠ 25.6%	⚠ 10.2%
ECONOMY	--	--
In civilian labor force, total, percent of population age 16+ years, 2016-2020	66.7%	63.0%
In civilian labor force, female, percent of population age 16+ years, 2016-2020	58.9%	58.4%
Total accommodation and food services sales, 2017 ($1,000)	11,039,101	938,237,077
Total healthcare and social assistance receipts/revenue, 2017 ($1,000)	32,073,432	2,527,903,275
Total transportation and warehousing receipts/revenue, 2017 (1,000)	26,597,641	895,225,411
Total retail sales, 2017 ($1,000)	53,089,247	4,949,601,481

POPULATION	PHOENIX, AZ	HOUSTON, TX	UNITED STATES
Population estimates, July 1, 2021 - (V2021)	⚠ 1,624,569	⚠ 2,288,250	⚠ 331,893,745
Population estimates base, April 1, 2020 - (V2021)	⚠ 1,607,739	⚠ 2,302,792	⚠ 331,449,281
Population, percent change - April 1, 2020 (V2021) (estimates base) to July 1, 2021	⚠ 1.0%	⚠ -0.6%	⚠ 0.1%
Population, Census, April 1, 2020	1,608,139	2,304,580	331,449,281
Population, Census, April 1, 2010	1,445,632	2,099,451	308,745,538
AGE AND SEX	--	--	--
Persons under 5 years, percent	⚠ 7.0%	⚠ 7.5%	⚠ 5.7%
Persons under 18 years, percent	⚠ 25.7%	⚠ 24.7%	⚠ 22.2%
Persons age 65 years and over, percent	⚠ 11.0%	⚠ 11.0%	⚠ 16.8%
Female persons, percent	⚠ 50.1%	⚠ 50.2%	⚠ 50.5%
RACE AND HISPANIC ORIGIN	--	--	--
White alone, percent	⚠ 68.2%	⚠ 51.5%	⚠ 75.8%
Black or African American alone, percent	⚠ 7.1%	⚠ 22.8%	⚠ 13.6%
American Indian and Alaska Native alone, percent	⚠ 2.0%	⚠ 0.3%	⚠ 1.3%
Asian alone, percent	⚠ 3.9%	⚠ 6.9%	⚠ 6.1%
Native Hawaiian and Other Pacific Islander alone, percent	⚠ 0.2%	⚠ 0.0%	⚠ 0.3%
Two or more races, percent	⚠ 8.3%	⚠ 7.0%	⚠ 2.9%
Hispanic or Latino, percent	⚠ 42.6%	⚠ 44.5%	⚠ 18.9%
White alone, not Hispanic or Latino, percent	⚠ 42.2%	⚠ 24.1%	⚠ 59.3%
POPULATION CHARACTERISTICS	--	--	--
Veterans, 2016-2020	73,226	69,023	17,835,456
Foreign-born persons, percent, 2016-2020	19.3%	28.9%	13.5%
HOUSING	--	--	--
Housing units, July 1, 2021, (V2021)	X	X	142,153,010
Owner-occupied housing unit rate, 2016-2020	55.6%	42.9%	64.4%
Median value of owner-occupied housing units, 2016-2020	$250,800	$186,800	$229,800
Median selected monthly owner costs—with a mortgage, 2016-2020	$1,490	$1,691	$1,621
Median selected monthly owner costs—without a mortgage, 2016-2020	$466	$541	$509
Median gross rent, 2016-2020	$1,100	$1,086	$1,096
Building permits, 2021	X	X	1,736,982
FAMILIES & LIVING ARRANGEMENTS	--	--	--
Households, 2016-2020	580,835	874,827	122,354,219
Persons per household, 2016-2020	2.82	2.61	2.60
Living in same house 1+ year ago, percent of persons age 1+ year, 2016-2020	83.9%	82.0%	86.2%
Language other than English spoken at home, percent of persons age 5+ years, 2016-2020	37.0%	48.4%	21.5%
COMPUTER AND INTERNET USE	--	--	--
Households with a computer, percent, 2016-2020	93.8%	91.5%	88.58%
Households with a broadband Internet subscription, percent, 2016-2020	86.0%	34.3%	32.9%

In the search bar at the top of the page, enter "Phoenix city," and the website will add a column with data for Phoenix beside the data for Houston and the US (see the graphic on the preceding page).

In comparing the two cities, you find that there are dramatically fewer foreign-born people living in Phoenix, and far fewer households speak a language other than English in the home. Total spending per capita in Phoenix is less than in Houston. Comparing these two columns of local data makes it much easier to select your first diverse market, and in this case, you and your team decide that Houston provides the greater opportunity for you to reach the Hispanic market with your product.

Since you know that people have a fairly long commute to work, you decide that radio ads are a good way to reach your new target customers, and since a large percentage of households in Houston speak a language other than English, you also know those ads should probably be in Spanish. However, the data also makes clear that most of your target customers use computers with broadband connections, so you also decide to reach them through social media.

The vast amount of data and robust search tools, provided by the website (*census.gov*), make it far easier to direct your marketing efforts efficiently and effectively toward the right diverse market. You can get as granular as you want with the Census data. Just play around with it, and you'll be amazed.

One of the most interesting filters for diverse marketing efforts is "foreign-born." As we all know, when immigrants come to this country, they sometimes struggle to assimilate into the patchwork quilt of American culture. It becomes easier for successive generations, but first-generation immigrants face many challenges.

Generally speaking, first-generation immigrants are still steeped in the language, culture, and lifestyle of their homeland. Consequently, they both need, and greatly appreciate, when companies embrace their culture and reach out to them in culturally-sensitive ways. If you demonstrate that you understand them, then you're more likely to win their business.

Census data makes it far easier to decide on your first diverse market segment, and the "foreign-born" filter is particularly helpful. However, you can access granular data on all sorts of things. Let's suppose you want to focus your marketing on the Hispanic community in Los Angeles. You can start broadly, then narrow it down to California. From there, you can further narrow it to Los Angeles County, and then Los Angeles itself.

This same process will work just as well for any city, whether it's a major metropolis or a small town. The Census data will go as geographically narrow as you need it to go, including as far down as a zip code. By exploring the data on the website, you can begin to identify a target market that you want to reach with your products and services. Ultimately, however, you don't want to get lost in the data.

The opportunity is vast. Don't wear yourself out trying to take it all in at once. Remember, you're just trying to choose one diverse market as a starting point. That will be enough to keep you busy for a good while, and one diverse market should be enough to achieve some amazing growth and profitability.

DIGGING A WELL, NOT A POND

When it comes to marketing to specific segments of a population, the key is to go deep with that market. Think of it as digging a well rather than creating a broad, shallow pond. Once you've identified a target market, you need to become part of the market so you understand the market better.

This takes work, but it's work that your competition probably isn't doing. Your target diverse market is ripe for harvesting, and you might find that you are the single player in that space.

Now that you're ahead of the curve, and you've found a diverse market to dominate, the next step is learn all about them so you can penetrate the market. The data you got from the US Census is actually secondary research. Your next step is to move on to the primary research: the culture itself.

STEP ONE KEY TAKEAWAYS

- When selecting a market, there's no better source of data-driven diversity marketing information than the US Census, which you can access for free at *census.gov*.

- By exploring the data on the website, you can begin to identify a target market that you will want to reach to sell your products and services. The Census data will go as geographically narrow as you need it to go.

- Remember, you're just trying to choose one diverse market as a starting point.

CHAPTER 4

STEP TWO: MARKET IMMERSION

"We have become not a melting pot but a beautiful mosaic. Different people, different beliefs, different yearnings, different hopes, different dreams."

—JIMMY CARTER

Learning about a culture and *really* getting to know the people is a challenge, and it will require a significant amount of change on your part. In fact, you're about to make a lifetime investment of time, effort, and resources. And just like purchasing a new home, you want to be intimately familiar with all of the details before taking the plunge.

Nobody buys a home sight unseen. They research it, tour the house, learn about the history of the house, get to know the surrounding neighborhood, and only when they feel well-informed and comfortable with the details do they finally sign the paperwork and make the down payment.

The same goes for your chosen diverse market. Before you can market to them effectively, you need to do the hard work of really getting to know them and understanding their history, language, hopes, needs, and desires. It's hard work, but fascinating! In this chapter, we'll look at some great ways that you can become immersed in your chosen diverse market.

FROM CONCEPT TO CONCRETE

It's time to get out of the office. You need to go out there and learn about your chosen market in person—immerse yourself with the people and the marketplace. Go to the centers of influence and connect with religious and community leaders. Learn the culture. See what and how they buy. Basically, get off the laptop and get out into the field.

There are actual events in every state or city, so if you want to get involved in cultural events, you can simply Google to find them. If you search online for "Hispanic events," you're going to get an exhaustive list of events you can attend and participate in.

This fieldwork isn't complicated, but it can be quite intimidating, especially in the beginning. However, getting out into your chosen diverse market is the only way to eliminate fear of the unknown. While you might be unsure at first, eventually you will feel right at home, and you'll become comfortable with a culture that might once have seemed foreign to you.

You just need to take that first intimidating step. The best way to start this journey is to set up a meeting and share a meal with someone from your selected market. The nuances of the personal interactions you have will give you a deeper look into their world, revealing aspects of the culture that you will miss out on if you only use Census data.

HOW TO MAKE CONTACT

Hopefully, you already know someone who comes from your chosen market. If so, you can simply invite that friend or acquaintance out for dinner. If not, the easiest way to find someone in your target market that you can meet with is through LinkedIn. Simply search for prominent surnames within your target market and reach out to prominent individuals.

For example, let's suppose you want to market to the Hispanic real estate market in Houston. First, you conduct a basic Google search to find the most common Hispanic surnames. You discover that there are ten major surnames in that community in the United States.

- Garcia: 1.2 million people
- Rodrigues: 1 million people
- Hernandez: 1 million people
- Martinez: 1 million people

- Lopez: 900,000 people
- Gonzales: 900,000 people
- Sanchez: 600,000 people
- Ramirez: 550,000 people
- Torres: 430,000 people
- Flores: 430,000 people

Next, you use LinkedIn's search box to find individuals with one of these common surnames who also meet your other criteria. In this case, you might search for "Garcia real estate agent Houston." What comes up should be a fairly large list of names. The same is true for ethnicity and industry.

Next, using your search results, you look for some particularly interesting or prominent individuals who meet your search criteria and reach out to them. A direct, friendly approach is best: "Hello, my name is So-and-So. My company has begun marketing to people in your culture and industry. I would love to meet with you sometime and learn about your own personal experiences. Would you be willing to get together for lunch sometime? My treat."

Once you've found someone who is willing to meet with you, prepare a series of questions ahead of time so you can make the most of your time together. Here is a list of recommended questions, but feel free to add your own industry-specific queries:

- How did you get started in the industry?
- What are your career aspirations?
- What are the biggest challenges you see in this indutry?
- What's the biggest sale you've ever made?
- What attracted you to the industry?
- Are your clients from the same diverse background as you?
- What would attract a person of your diverse background to another organization?
- How do you develop clients?
- How do you identify potential buyers, sellers, and renters?
- What social media do you use (e.g., LinkedIn, Facebook, WeChat, Instagram)?
- What country is your family from?

- Do you have a specific dialect that you speak at home or in the community?
- Is there a geographical concentration of people from your diverse background that live in this area?
- What are the major holidays celebrated by your community? How are these holidays celebrated?
- What festivals or community events are prevalent in your diverse community?
- Do you prefer working for an organization owned by someone from your diverse background?
- Where do you buy your groceries? (I particularly like this question because if there is a certain ethnic supermarket in the area, it indicates that there is a large population of that ethnic group nearby.)
- Are there specific houses of worship that are frequented by the Hispanic community?

THE POWER OF A CONVERSATION

I recently had dinner with a young man who is a Chinese immigrant. By asking a series of simple questions, I discovered that his family came to America when he was twelve years old. His father had already been in the States for six years prior to his family's arrival. He was preparing a life for them by applying for a green card, finding a place to live, working and saving money, and so on.

His father faced many challenges during those six years. He barely spoke any English. He couldn't get a mortgage. He struggled to build credit. And somehow, despite it all, he had to figure out how to survive in a brand-new country and culture.

At the time of our dinner, the man's father was sixty-five years old. He'd started working as a dishwasher, but he worked his way up to becoming a cook. Eventually, he opened his own Chinese takeout restaurant (the kind of folksy place that doesn't accept credit cards, never has, and probably never will), and over the last fifteen years, the family's lifestyle has flourished. They've been able to purchase a home. In fact, the family has purchased three homes over the years.

"How was your family able to buy three homes?" I asked. "Earlier, you mentioned that your father was unable to acquire a mortgage."

The young man explained to me a certain communal ideology that exists in the Chinese-American community, where individuals will lend money to one another. Just imagine what a financial services company that was seeking to penetrate the Chinese-American market could do with that information.

Upon further questioning, I learned that he was one of three siblings, which he said is about average for his culture, and they reside in multi-generational housing, with the grandparents, parents, children, and grandchildren all living under one roof. I also learned that in Chinese-American families, many first-generation fathers and grandfathers never become fluent in English. The children translate for them. That means, among other things, a company could potentially market to each generation differently at the same time (one message for the non-English speaking parents and grandparents, another for the bilingual children and grandchildren).

He also told me that his family donated heavily to their local religious organization. They value education very highly and prefer to eat at home in order to save money. However, the question that provided the most intriguing answer was one I did not expect. Almost off the cuff, I asked him, "If there was a soccer game between the United States and China, who would you cheer for?"

Surprisingly, despite having lived in this country for more than twenty years, he told me that he would proudly support the Chinese team. This suggests that many Chinese-American people, especially among first- and second-generation immigrants, feel more *Chinese* than *American*. That's an incredibly important insight when creating messaging for that market.

I would have discovered none of this if I hadn't sat down over dinner and had a conversation with someone from that culture. These kinds of experiential truths are not readily apparent from reading Census data or statistics. You have to step into the community, get to know the people, and learn from them directly. Immerse yourself in your primary target diverse market.

CULTURAL KNOWLEDGE IS POWER

Depending on your personality, it's not always easy to reach out to strangers and try to engage them in conversation. However, your efforts are going to provide you with a solid base of cultural knowledge about your selected market—knowledge that the majority of your competition probably won't have. This will give you a distinct advantage when it comes to crafting messaging that resonates powerfully with your target market. You will speak the language, not just in terms of vocabulary.

Accept the fact that it will often be uncomfortable. We usually avoid having awkward conversations with complete strangers from other cultures, but it's a paradigm that needs to change. Take the time to analyze Census data, use a simple Google search to identify common surnames in your target market, then find individuals who meet your criteria on LinkedIn. From there, you can simply begin inviting people to sit down with you and discuss their cultural experiences.

Over time, after you've done this repeatedly, you will become somewhat of an expert in that diverse market, which will not only give you an advantage, but it might just give you the power to become the sole provider of your products and services in your selected marketplace. The power of knowing and understanding your ideal client in this way can't be overstated.

Using your newfound knowledge, you can now start thinking through the process of how you will market and communicate your business to this group. Decide which social media platforms you're going to use. Are there specific platforms that your target market seems to prefer? For example, I learned that certain Asian communities in America use WeChat heavily.

What is WeChat? It's a Chinese messaging, social media, and mobile payment app that was started in 2011 and has become the world's largest standalone mobile app. In 2018, there were over 1 billion market users. The app is available in seventeen languages, allows for text, voice, and broadcast messaging, video conferencing, video games, and is available in simplified Chinese, traditional Chinese, Japanese, Korean, Spanish, Malay, Thai, and Vietnamese. If you are targeting the Asian market, this is an incredible social media platform.

However, if you're targeting the Hispanic market, Hispanic people traditionally lean toward utilizing

WhatsApp. They use WhatsApp more than Instagram and Twitter. There are more than 10 million Hispanic users on WhatsApp than Instagram, and three times more users than on Twitter because data costs are less, messaging is encrypted, and it is popular with relatives in their home countries.

Figure out how you're going to change your social media profiles to communicate the fact that you are embracing the market. Identify which community events you're going to attend, and which community influencers you will add to your contacts. Make a plan for recognizing significant cultural holidays in a way that is respectful and sensitive.

All diverse segments can be penetrated, but it's important, as you start your journey, not to be looked upon as a gold digger who is only interested in leveraging them for revenue. A good place to start is to acknowledge key diverse holidays and their significance to the community. Communicate that you embrace holidays through relevant social media platforms like LinkedIn, Instagram, Facebook, WeChat, WhatsApp, and Twitter.

Key holidays to acknowledge include Martin Luther King Jr. Day, the first day of Ramadan, Passover, Lunar New Year, Yom Kippur, Cinco de Mayo, Black History Month, Juneteenth, Dragon Boat Festival, and LGBTQ Pride Month. The significance of each of these to their respective community can be found with a Google search. Post a short message for each of them on all of your social media accounts.

The following pages show some examples of posts I made for cultural holidays in 2022.

As you become intimate with your target market, you will overcome any uncertainty you might have about understanding a different culture and community. In turn, you will gain the confidence you need to keep moving forward. Remember how I said it's a lot like buying a house? You don't just blindly pick a house off a list. Rather, you spend some time investigating the property, collecting the broad details online, and then gathering the finer points by meeting with current homeowners and possible neighbors. You might even go as far as to stop by the local school and police station.

Vince Vitiello · You
President at New America Marketing
2mo · 🌐   • • •

New America Marketing would like to wish everyone a happy Pride Month. "Openness may not completely disarm prejudice, but it's a good place to start" - Jason Collins

#pride2022 #pridemonth #lgbtqcommunity #celebrate #unity

🏷 with **New America Marketing**

Vince Vitiello · You
President at New America Marketing
4mo · 🌐

Wishing all who celebrate Ramadan a peaceful and fulfilling month #RamadanMubarak #RamadanKareem

Ramadan Kareem

May this Ramadan bring joy, health and wealth to you.

Strength Insurance Brokerage

Vince Vitiello · You
President at New America Marketing
6mo · 🌐

We all should know Dr. King's greatest quote at this point but here is a lesser known one, a great question that we at NAM ask ourselves constantly:

"Life's most persistent and urgent question is, what are you doing for others?"

We look forward to doing more for others this year.

Vince Vitiello · You
President at New America Marketing
8mo · 🌐   · · ·

Wishing you a warm and wonderful Hannukah filled with love and laughs.

New America Marketing
40 followers
8mo · 🌐

As the holiday season continues, we would like to wish our Jewish friends a Happy Hannukah!

Only after you've done your due diligence, when you feel like you finally have a very clear idea of the house and surrounding neighborhood, do you feel confident enough to take the plunge and make that big investment. The same goes for your target market. It is well worth the time, effort, and resources to research the market upfront, get to know people from the community, and learn as much as you can about them. That way, you're less likely to make a communication blunder when you begin reaching out with your marketing.

This approach appears very tactical, but imagine you're the CEO of a large firm, and you're discussing with your team the in-depth knowledge you've learned just by having a personal meeting with a leader from your selected market. Your team will be very interested and really on board with your commitment.

And to repeat, when you take the time to immerse in your target market, it puts you far ahead of most of your competition. At this point, you're ready to start attracting and retaining clients and customers from your chosen market. There's one way, and one way alone, to do that: by creating value.

STEP TWO KEY TAKEAWAYS

- Before you can market to your chosen diverse market effectively, you need to get to know them and understand their history, language, hopes, needs, and desires.

- Begin by setting up a meeting and sharing a meal with someone from your selected market. If you don't already know someone from that market, reach out to someone on LinkedIn.

- Leave the office and go out there to experience your chosen market in person. Immerse yourself with the people and in places. Go to the centers of influence and connect with religious and community leaders. Learn the culture. See what and how they buy. Google for cultural events you can get involved in. Appeal to them by being aware of their special holidays and posting on the best social media platforms specifically used by your target market.

CHAPTER 5

STEP THREE: BUILDING YOUR UNIQUE VALUE PROPOSITION

"Focusing on the customer makes
a company more resilient."

—JEFF BEZOS

The concept of creating a value proposition is relatively new to the world of marketing, credited to Michael Lanning and Edward Michaels of McKinsey & Company. The idea is that a business should be able to make a clear, simple statement about the benefits, both tangible and intangible, that the company provides. Put more simply, a value proposition states succinctly *why* a customer should turn to you.

Uber's value proposition for riders is: "The smartest way to get around." For Apple, it's: "The experience *is* the product." For the popular workplace messaging app, Slack, it's: "Be more productive at work with less effort."

With a value proposition, you deliver, communicate, and acknowledge to your customer what your business promises to do, and you give the customer an expectation of how that promise will be experienced and delivered. Just about every business in every industry has a value proposition, though sometimes it's not clearly identified. The problem is that your typical value proposition will never attract customers from diverse markets.

In fact, the value proposition of the average business, no matter the industry, has a "one size fits all" approach to communicating what the company delivers that fails to differentiate between various kinds of customers and customer segments. If you're going to attract customers from a diverse market, you need a value proposition that speaks to them directly.

WHAT COMPANIES THINK THEY HAVE

When it comes to your target market, your value proposition needs to do a number of things. First, it should identify your target market's main problems. Then, it should clearly define how the benefits of your product or service solves those problems. In other words, it states what makes your product valuable specifically for your target market. You need to connect that value to your customer.

Finally, it needs to differentiate you in a way that positions your company as the preferred provider of this value for this target market. And it needs to do all of this succinctly. No easy feat. Much thought needs to be exercised to accomplish this.

Now, when I speak to CEOs and CMOs about their value propositions, they usually claim they've already done all of the things mentioned in the previous paragraphs, and they're eager to share with me their four- or five-point value proposition. But I've done enough consulting that I can usually guess what their value proposition is going to say before they ever show it to me. In my experience, most value propositions look something like this:

- "We have high integrity in our organization."
- "Our customer service is the best."
- "Our products are superior to other carriers and companies."
- "Our technology connects our consumers to our product."
- "Our culture is just wonderful."

Do any of these sound familiar? They should. They're incredibly common. In fact, there's a good chance that your company's value proposition says something along these lines.

When I'm consulting with someone, and they present me with a value proposition like this, I usually follow up by asking them, "In addition to this statement, how would you attract consumers from a diverse group to your company?" And I'm usually met with silence, because most business leaders *just don't know*.

I'm not suggesting that the above list of value items are bad. It's not bad to have high integrity or superior products or a wonderful culture. But they're commonplace, broad, and add nothing specific to attract a diverse clientele.

The mindset behind these kinds of generic statements is usually something along the lines of, "Our value proposition is so good, it will attract any customer we want." And the truth is, you *might* attract some diverse customers, but you will never dominate these markets or gain the revenue opportunity unless you focus and segment your value proposition.

Similar to you, I also run a business, New America Marketing. To me, it's quite simple to connect with my clients' greatest need–how to drive additional sales revenue–so what differentiates me from someone else they could do business with? My simple story is this: people ask me how my company can help, and they ask me what my company does. They're always surprised when I respond this way:

"I create marketing strategies for companies to help obtain customers that don't look like me; more specifically, Asian-, Hispanic-, African-American, and other diverse groups." That's my value proposition.

COMMUNICATING VALUE THE RIGHT WAY

Suppose you have a financial services company, and you decide to target the foreign-born Asian market (a market that is currently exploding in the US). In terms of products and services, let's suppose you provide insurance and investment advice. As you explore your target market, you look at your competitors and see generic value propositions like those listed earlier. Seeing a huge opportunity, you decide to craft a value proposition that will appeal to this specific diverse market. How do you go about doing that?

First, as we discussed above, *you consider the consumers' main problems*, which for first-generation immigrants are many. Their biggest problem is a lack of education about the financial industry. Most foreign-born individuals have a basic awareness of Social Security, health insurance, life insurance, Medicare, Medicaid, and so on, but they lack intimate knowledge about them. Consequently, they often miss out on financial help that is readily available to them.

Another big problem for most foreign-born immigrants is figuring out how to easily and affordably send money to their families back in the homeland. Indeed, many people immigrate in the first place in order to provide for struggling families back home, but they don't always know the best ways to get the money to them.

A competitor using generic messaging would treat these customers as if they had been born into the system and understood the basics of American finances and economics. However, you have gotten to know this diverse market, and you're making plans to address their specific needs. As part of that process, you are developing foundational educational materials for the market that will bring them up to speed on government programs, economic opportunities, and affordable money wiring services. You can communicate this succinctly in your value proposition and marketing materials.

Now, which company do you suppose is going to win more business from the growing market of foreign-born Asian immigrants? The answer is obvious, but we're just getting started.

Second, once you've identified the major problems your target market is dealing with, *you need to consider their primary language*. In this case, it's Mandarin. Although many foreign-born immigrants can speak English, they often prefer to use their native language in everyday life. That means when they have to choose between a bilingual company or an English-only company, they are far more likely to do business with a bilingual company.

So, your financial services company decides to double down on marketing in Mandarin, and you also hire some Mandarin-speaking employees at each level of the organization. Not only do you want team members who can speak Mandarin on the frontline in direct interactions with customers, you ultimately want team members internally who speak and understand the language to help make communication decisions.

A few years ago, I picked up four of my Chinese-American colleagues at the Minneapolis airport. All of my colleagues were born in Hong Kong, but they've been in this country for at least thirty years. Their kids were born in the United States and attended college here. The four colleagues were completely assimilated into American culture. However, as soon as they got in the car, they began to speak Cantonese. Maybe it was because they feel more comfortable with their native language, or maybe they were trying to hide something from me!

Third, you begin *reaching out to individuals* who meet your criteria for your ideal customers in your selected market, and you begin meeting with them to discuss their experiences. Along the way, you discover that this community tends to live in multi-generational households, so you're able to tweak your marketing to reach everyone from the children to the grandparents. Meanwhile, your competition is completely unaware of this aspect of the community, so they don't address it in their messaging.

Last, but certainly not least, you now have a deep understanding of the citizenship struggles that consumers in your target market deal with. You've heard their stories about dealing with green cards and tax

IDs. You know about all of the financial problems that non-citizens face. This knowledge enables you to *quickly identify which customers qualify for your various services*, and it clarifies how you can educate others, so they quickly become qualified as well. Needless to say, your competition doesn't stand a chance in this market!

So, in the end, your financial services company expertly connects the value you provide to the specific problems of people in this diverse market. You craft a value proposition that differentiates you from your competitors, and as a result, you quickly become the dominant player in that market.

I've seen this exact scenario play out many times in different industries. There's power in a value proposition when it communicates in a clear and compelling way to a specific diverse market.

DOMINATING YOUR SELECTED MARKET

So, how are you going to create your compelling value proposition that will attract consumers in your chosen market? If you've done your research, you should have a clear idea now of the specific problems that people in your market struggle with. How are you going to connect your products and services to those problems?

There are some common ways to do this. You get to choose which ones you will use. For example, will you create a website, marketing, and educational materials in the native language of your market? Will you run a social media outreach program or start a podcast to share the testimonies of diverse customers?

Maybe you should consider hiring bilingual customer service workers or providing multiple language options on your 800 number? Perhaps you should hire more bilingual employees across the board, even drawing people from the community itself?

These are the kinds of options you have to consider if you're going to communicate value to a diverse market. Knowing your market allows you to make smart decisions that will resonate with consumers. Before long, you should have a full suite of bilingual sales collateral. You might be hosting charitable events in the community.

When you know *how* you're going to provide value to your target market, you can then create a succinct and memorable value proposition that communicates it. Consider Airbnb's value proposition as a good example of how to do this: "Airbnb exists to create a world where anyone can belong anywhere, providing healthy travel that is local, authentic, diverse, inclusive, and sustainable."

Along the way, you will become the dominant provider in the market, because you took the time to create a value proposition that is focused and caters to your chosen diverse market more than your competitors. Use social media to constantly remind your selected market of your progress regarding your value proposition. Anytime you add an additional aspect of your value proposition, communicate it to your client base with pictures, stories, and events.

Now, if you're a savvy business owner, then you're probably thinking something along these lines right about now: "All of this sounds great, but *how much is it going to cost?*" That's a fair question, and I'm not going to lie to you.

It won't be cheap!

However, the trick is to look at it as an investment that is almost guaranteed to produce massive growth rather than a cost that only makes a dent in your profits. If you're not yet convinced of the growth potential of investment in diverse markets, let's look at the actual numbers.

STEP THREE KEY TAKEAWAYS

- Your value proposition should be a clear, simple statement about the benefits, both tangible and intangible, that your product or service provides.

- Your value proposition needs to identify your target market's main problems and clearly define how the benefits of your product or service solves those problems.

- When crafting your value proposition, first consider the consumers' main problems— understanding that first-generation immigrants have many—then consider their primary language. Reach out to individuals in your selected market and begin meeting with them to discuss their experiences.

CHAPTER 6

STEP FOUR: DOLLARS IN = 10X GROWTH

"We know that diversity can sometimes be more uncomfortable because things are less familiar—but it gets the best results."

—MEGAN SMITH

The year was 2012. I had some extra cash (around $10,000) that I was looking to park somewhere and let grow. Apple stock at the time was on the rise, and I was considering investing my funds with the company.

After a bit of back and forth, I ultimately decided on another investment—which did well enough, but I think you know where this is headed. That $10,000 that I could have placed in Apple back then would be worth about $110,000 today.

There's no getting around it. I missed out on an enormous investment opportunity. To be fair, I had *no idea* I was missing out on a chance to 10X my original investment. I was not clued in to the fact that Apple was about to take off in a big way.

Here's the thing: diverse markets have the same potential. They are growing at an amazing rate across the country, their buying power is growing even faster, and they're just waiting for companies to court them. Hopefully, by now, I've done a good enough job of showing you how America is changing and how diverse markets are on the rise (exploding, actually). The potential is huge!

In one major financial services company, when I was the chief marketing and distribution officer, I presented to my distribution about the changing marketplace. The group was 100 percent White, and the CEO took me aside and reminded me that I was not the diversity champion. However, I was passionate about diversity and knew it was the future of the company. A few years later, I left that firm, and the company has experienced 10X growth mainly because of their commitment to diverse markets.

The opportunity is there. It's crystal clear. If you wisely invest today by developing a segment of your business that focuses on diverse markets, you may very well gain what I missed out on: a 10X increase of your investment.

Remember, Apple's tremendous stock growth didn't happen overnight. In fact, it took about ten years. It would have required a little patience on my part if I wanted to enjoy that 10X return on my investment. The same is probably true of your current business. How many years has it taken you to get where you are today? Very few businesses experience overnight success. Usually, it takes time, a long-term investment, and a lot of hard work.

The same is true of investing in diverse markets. You're probably not going to experience overnight success. You are developing a new segment of your business, and that's going to take an investment of time and money, just like it did when you built the main parts of your business.

I share this because I've seen too many people give up too quickly when investing in diverse markets. They develop unrealistic expectations about when, and how soon, they'll see results. Can you imagine if I'd invested that $10,000 in Apple then pulled all of the money out a year later because it wasn't growing fast enough? Typically, during budget constraints, the first initiatives to be discontinued are the broad visionary ideas.

You're probably not the same as you were when you first started your business. You've learned, grown, and changed along the way. Maybe your company has been in business for decades. Here's the good news. While entering a diverse market won't be an overnight success—probably not even a "one-year wonder"—it also won't be the same kind of slog that you experienced in the early days of your business.

Since you've learned and grown so much since your business started, you have acquired systems, capital, and experience that you didn't have before. You also now have a vision to drive everything forward. In short, you can do a lot more a lot faster now than you could in the beginning, so you should be able to build up momentum in your diverse marketing efforts faster than you did when you launched your business.

The reward is there, and all of the investment is going to be well worth it. The data and statistics make that clear, and you should see it for yourself by now. If you're ready and willing to make this happen, then it's time to gear up for battle. Remind yourself to be patient through this journey.

MENTAL MANAGEMENT

When you decide to enter diverse markets, you'll be making an investment of time and money, and as with any business plan, you need to decide how much you're willing to devote to this effort. A word of caution: go slow! Let your dollar investment grow in proportion to the revenue you receive from your selected market.

This is a mistake I see all too often. A CEO will see all of the data about the growth of diverse markets, they'll get a sense of what they're missing out on, and they'll start seeing dollar signs. "Dump everything into diverse markets now," they'll say. "We see huge potential in diverse markets, and we want to reap the rewards!"

Now, that attitude is not a bad thing. On the contrary, having a strong vision about the growth potential in diverse markets is essential if you want your team to make the long-term commitment.

However, you can't simply start dumping vast amounts of your company profits into diverse markets right away, expecting immediate returns. I've seen a few CEOs invest *too much too fast*, and when those returns don't happen quickly, they get discouraged and frustrated. It's important to realize that this is going to be a slow process initially and will take some time to build momentum.

Start small, be patient, and keep at it. Don't overspend, and don't overpromise. That's the mindset you need to have if you want to get to those exponential returns.

Another common mistake that companies make is to assume a few minor tweaks to their current value proposition will deliver results in their target market. Small changes will produce small returns, if they produce any returns at all. You really have to delve into the culture and experiences of your target market so you can communicate with them in a powerful way.

Investing too much too fast or not investing enough—both of these mistakes cause leaders to cut their initiatives short, and they miss out on all of that amazing growth. As we all know from experience, the marketing budget is usually the first thing to get cut during a financial crisis, and an initiative like "diverse marketing" that seems experimental to "non-diverse" leaders will be on the chopping block before just about anything else.

Avoid both extremes. Settle it in your mind that this is going to take a significant investment of time and money, but that investment is going to happen over time. You need to be mentally prepared for the long haul. I can't emphasize this enough. To get my 10X return on Apple stock in 2012, I would have had to wait ten years. That's a long time, but it would have been worth it. I wish I had made the investment, added to it over time, and stuck with it.

Now is the right time to get involved in diverse markets. We're right in the middle of the population explosion. Don't miss out. Commit to the long-term investment, be willing to take it slow at first, and give it all of the time and hard work it takes to *do it right*.

HOW MUCH WILL IT COST?

So, what is all of this going to cost? How much money should you expect to invest in your diverse marketing initiative? Fortunately, the initial financial investment will be cheap, even free. The website (*census.gov*) is available to the public free of charge, and "buying" your ideal client will cost pennies on the dollar in the grand scheme of things.

Recently, a CEO client said to me, after discussing with him the potential of various diverse markets, "This is the greatest day in our company's history because of the diversity opportunity that's in front of us."

Here are a few more "free investments" you can make to start building momentum in your diverse marketing efforts:

- A simple PowerPoint presentation to create awareness within your company about your diverse marketing initiative (e.g., a review of the data from your Census analysis and meeting with people in your selected community)
- Creating a business plan for your diverse marketing initiative
- Adding LinkedIn contacts of people in your selected market
- Posting on social media to show your involvement in the community
- Baselining your progress in diverse marketing to track your progress
- Researching and selecting your next market

Other than a bit of time, you probably haven't made any significant investment up to this point. Now, you can begin to wisely select a few things to spend money on. Remember, don't overdo it. Take it slow at first. Here are a few ways to spend your initial financial investment:

- Develop collateral specific to your chosen market
- Translate your current collateral into the language or language of that market
- Develop a bilingual or multilingual website
- Hire key bilingual staff (particularly in Human Resources, Customer Service, and Sales)
- Purchase segmented customer lists (organized by gender, ethnicity, age, etc.)
- Attend or host cultural community events
- Get involved in charitable endeavors; become a board of director member in charities that matter to the community
- Develop video and other kinds of content
- Travel to visit the community

You don't need millions of dollars to get started, and the new diverse marketing segment of your business doesn't need to look like your current marketing model.

It certainly doesn't need to be as big or robust while it's in the initial stages.

As I have said, take it slow and ramp up your efforts as you gain traction in the market. If you do that, you will achieve the success that I've been talking about.

SPEARHEADING THE INITIATIVE

So, what's your biggest investment going to be? Time. You will need to spend some part of each day researching the market, interacting with the community, and leading your team to do the same. This is why it's so important for leaders to have vision and passion when it comes to diverse marketing.

You're going to have to make some hard decisions about how much time to take away from developing your core business. Many leaders are tempted to delegate their diverse marketing initiative entirely to their team, but I strongly urge you to be centrally involved! When leaders aren't at the heart of a diverse marketing effort, it's a death knell for the initiative. You will never successfully penetrate the market unless you lead the way.

Why? Because your people are going to be wracked with doubt and indecision about the effort. They'll worry that the process is taking too long. People tend to be afraid of the unknown anyway, so if they don't have a visionary leader directing their efforts, they are going to be resistant to change.

Diving head-first into a new culture is just about the biggest change you can make, and there may be some degree of discomfort and awkwardness. People will worry about making unintentional mistakes or cultural faux pas that get them in trouble with the culture. And if we're being brutally honest, there are probably also some people in your company who have prejudices against your selected market. "Oh, that community has low income. They're not worth the effort."

Recently, I met with a very senior executive of a property and casualty insurance company, who at one time had a keen interest in diverse markets. However, his most recent experiences with these markets has not been positive. In the property and casualty business, while topline revenues could be very exciting, these companies measure their success on the amount of losses they take in a particular market. His short-term experiences were not positive, and so he lost interest in pursuing diverse market.

However, another company that I've dealt with in a similar geographic marketplace has doubled its size because of their focus on the Chinese market. This company's CEO has taken the time to figure out how to work around the losses the other company had experienced and focused on accepting better business and rejecting certain business that might cause problems.

Only a visionary leader who is truly committed to the effort can break through these fears, tensions, and prejudices. You need to be the leader who spearheads this initiative.

A VISION OF THE FUTURE

So, what kind of ROI (return on investment) can you expect on your diverse marketing efforts? ROI is a performance measure used to evaluate the efficiency or profitability of an investment. With that in mind, here's a word of warning about analyzing the ROI of diverse marketing. If you compare the returns from diverse marketing with the ROI of your core business, you're bound to be sorely disappointed. That doesn't mean it's not worth the effort or that it's not paying off.

How can that be? Let's use the stock market as an example. Your core business is similar to investing in Coca-Cola: a predictable investment that's ongoing with steady, predictable growth. Investing in a diverse market is more like investing in a successful startup that has some cutting edge new tech, which means it is probably going to experience hockey stick growth.

In other words, your initial ROI will be small, and growth will seem slow. However, at some point in the future, when you've invested enough and spread deep roots in the community, you will experience a sudden meteoric rise with dramatic returns. We can use the example of Apple's growth during those ten years as an example of what hockey stick growth looks like.[14]

---

14 "Apple Inc (AAPL) Stock 10 Year History." n.d. Netcials. https://www. netcials.com/stock-10-year-history/AAPL-Apple-Inc/.

APPLE INC. (AAPL) STOCK 10 YEAR HISTORY

There's also the example of Netflix during their first
seven years of growth.

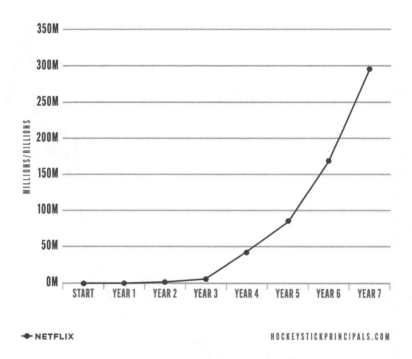

To get to the point where slow, gradual growth
becomes exponential growth, you need a leader with
vision who understands how developing these diverse
markets is going to pay off. A leader with the skills and
business sense to see the initiative through.

That leader is going to start creating a baseline that the company can use to measure success. And as the company sees more business coming from those diverse markets, they should celebrate the milestones because that's going to help employees catch hold of the grand vision.

I'll say it again. A huge opportunity is there just waiting to be realized. With the right application of time and resources, guided by a visionary leader, your investment has great potential to become your "hockey stick" ROI. You just need patience.

Once you've done your homework to identify a market, and you've embraced the mindset you need to make the commitment, you're ready to get into the nitty-gritty details of creating a strategic, actionable plan for reaching people in the market. We'll look at how you do that next.

STEP FOUR KEY TAKEAWAYS

- You need to decide how much you're willing to devote to this effort. Take it slow, and let your dollar investment grow as you gain traction in the market. Remember to be patient. It takes time.

- Use "free investments" to start building momentum in your diverse marketing efforts.

- Stay centrally involved. Your people are going to be wracked with doubt and indecision, and only a visionary leader who is truly committed to the effort can break through these fears, tensions, and prejudices.

CHAPTER 7

STEP FIVE: BUILDING YOUR STRATEGIC PLAN

"A goal without a plan is just a wish."

—LARRY ELDER

If you've made it this far, hopefully, you're convinced that the face of America is changing. The lack of competition in diverse markets, I hope, has fully shown you just how much opportunity is available. Maybe you are now at the point where you have done your research and selected one diverse market as a starting point,

and you're working on becoming intimately familiar with that culture and community, as well as their
unique experiences, challenges, and needs.

If so, you are leaps and bounds ahead of most other
companies in your industry. With your chosen market, you should also know by now precisely what level
of investment you're going to make in this endeavor in
terms of time, money, and resources. Once you've done
all of that, you're ready for the next vital part of the
diverse marketing journey: creating your strategic plan.

You've heard this one, so say it with me: *failing to plan
is planning to fail*. We can also say that a vision without a strategy is just a dream. If you want to attract and
retain consumers from your target market, you need
a plan that is executable, with concrete steps that turn
the dream into a reality. Otherwise, it's just an empty
idea that won't go anywhere.

PUTTING IT ON PAPER

There are a few significant benefits to creating a strategic plan for your diverse marketing initiative. For

one thing, it gets all of your team on the same page. I strongly recommend putting the plan down on paper. It's not enough for the strategic plan to merely exist in your head. Make it tangible, something that people can see with their own eyes, because that makes it easier for them to get behind it. A plan in writing demonstrates a big commitment by leadership.

Your strategic plan should identify your competition, if any. It must also define your unique value proposition. It should establish the steps you're going to take to target your customers, with concrete milestones to track your progress toward your ROI.

To use our earlier example, let's suppose you're trying to decide between Phoenix or Houston as your target market for opening up ten new real estate offices to serve bilingual Hispanic brokers and consumers. Let's now develop a broad strategic business plan.

☑ *Define Your Target Market*
Start by defining your target market, sharing the findings of your primary and secondary research, including the age, income, ethnicity, language(s), and

geographical locations of the markets you want to penetrate. Consolidate all of these findings into a digestible format that can be delivered to your team.

During our business strategy discussions with our team, we set out to research and decide on which geographical market would be the most fertile for our project. We looked at two: Houston and Phoenix. We wanted the geographical area to be near our home office, and we wanted to focus on one geographical area rather than a national rollout of our marketing strategy.

First, we needed to become familiar with the Hispanic market, so we conducted primary research by utilizing LinkedIn and contacts we'd made with Hispanic real estate brokers in both of our markets. We were able to uncover culturally specific information from our individual meetings with people in the community (refer to our checklist of questions in Chapter Four under the heading "How to Make Contact").

Second, we used *census.gov* to conduct demographic research into these two markets, and we were able to reveal that Houston and Phoenix are both great locations for our strategic plan. In both markets, over

40 percent of the population is of Hispanic descent. However, between the two, Houston's foreign-born population is 30 percent, while Phoenix's is only 20 percent.

Third, we also discovered that in 40 percent of the households in Houston the primary language spoken at home is a language other than English, but that is the case in only 30 percent of the Phoenix households. Last but not least, over 90 percent of both markets have a computer in the home and in both instances nearly 85 percent have broadband internet. From all of this information, our team has decided that while both markets have enormous potential, Houston was best suited for our initiative.

☑ *What's Our Product or Goal?*

Next, identify your product or the goal you want to achieve. We want to become the largest real estate agency in Houston catering exclusively to the Hispanic, bilingual, foreign-born buyers and brokers. We want to contact 200 brokers over the next twelve months, and we want to establish ten retail real estate offices in the greater Houston area. Be specific and be focused.

☑ *Identify Your Competition*

You can conduct an exhaustive study to find out how much competition you have in the market. In this instance, I Googled "Hispanic real estate brokers in Houston" and found that there really are no Hispanic brokerages in the market. It's actually quite easy to find out what competitors are doing to reach your target demographic. While I conducted only a cursory search, a simple Google search can reveal how much competition you will be facing in your new market, if any.

☑ *Create a Presentation*

The next step is to communicate your findings to your team. Every team member needs to know everything that you now know about your target market, so they can get as excited about reaching it as you are. It's up to you as a leader to generate that excitement and enthusiasm. There are going to be at least a few doubters, so be ready to quell any resistance by creating a brief, compelling presentation about why the company is targeting this market. You need buy-in from your full team.

You can create a presentation about your diverse marketing initiative for your team, investors, and board that will get them excited and help them understand the project. Here's what should go into the presentation:

- Overall demographics: primary and secondary research
- Demonstrating your findings from *census.gov*
- The goals of the project
- Who your competitions is
- Why this is important for you as a business initiative
- The metrics of how you will evaluate progress
- Expectations for the team
- What your new value proposition is going to be
- Your investment/financials

☑ *Value Proposition*

Write your value proposition simply and succinctly. For our Houston marketing initiatives, the steps to satisfy our new value proposition will include software in Spanish and English that identifies would-be buyers and sellers of property. It will also include specific radio spots (in English and Spanish) on Spanish radio stations and a broad social media blitz including WhatsApp and Facebook. We will conduct bilingual educational seminars for potential buyers that will include instructions on finances, mortgages, estimating closing costs, and how to evaluate properties. We will also seek proprietary lending sources that focus on the Hispanic market and Green Card holders, and we will develop a bilingual website.

☑ The Investment/Metrics/ROI

When clarifying your investment for the initiative, it's important to list the specific costs for advertising, social media, and hiring a bilingual social media expert, as well as the costs for printing and translation of collateral, website development, and investments for community events.

Create a one-, two-, and three-year projection for your investment, a one-, two-, and three-year projection for your revenue, a one-, two-, and three-year projection for your profit, and a one-, two-, and three-year projection for your return on investment. Also, identify the key personnel who will be responsible for the execution of the plan, their bio, and why they are the person or team who has been chosen.

FOLLOWING THROUGH

Your diverse marketing initiative began with a vision. Now, you have crafted a strategic plan using real data and you've put it down on paper where every team member can see it and begin to wrap their head around it.

As a leader, you've done the hard work of communicating that plan and getting the team on your side. From this point on, your commitment will be the driving force that ensures your team continues to realize the strategic plan and works fervishly to dominate the new market.

Next is where the rubber meets the road. It's time to execute the plan!

STEP FIVE KEY TAKEAWAYS

- Create a strategic plan for your diverse marketing initiative and put it down on paper. To do that:

- Define your target market, sharing the findings of your primary and secondary research.

- Identify your product or the goal you want to achieve.

- Identify your competitors, if any, and what they are doing to reach your target demographic.

- Create a presentation about your diverse marketing initiative for your team, investors, and board.

- Write a simple and succinct value proposition.

- Clarify your investment for the initiative, including specific costs and one-, two-, and three-year projections for investment, revenue, profit, and ROI.

CHAPTER 8

STEP SIX: MARKET READY
TRACKING YOUR PROGRESS

"What gets measured, gets managed."

—PETER DRUCKER

Practice time is at an end. It's time to step out on the field and implement your finely tuned plan. But a plan doesn't do you much good if you can't measure your success. In any professional sport, there's a scoreboard, so every player on your team knows how close they are to victory. You need to do the same for your diverse marketing initiative.

Measuring success starts with creating a baseline. That means scheduling regular check-ins to determine where you are right now and contrasting it with where you want to be. How much progress have you made? You need to be able to answer this question so you know exactly how your investment is doing.

Think of it like a rain gauge. A rain gauge measures the amount of rainfall per day, week, or month. By measuring your progress with regular check-ins, you know how much you've accomplished and how much more remains to be done. That gives you the information you need to keep taking action.

CREATING THE BASELINE

The first step in understanding your success is creating the datum, your starting point—or as I like to call it, your baseline. This initial reference point allows you to see your progress and perform the necessary "calculus" for your financial reports and tracking. To be clear, setting your initial baseline isn't going to be straightforward or the easiest of tasks because you need to know exactly how much business you are already receiving from your selected market. That might require some market research.

This is important because you don't want to mistakenly attribute some of your new initiative's progress to transactions you're already making. If you aren't sure how to conduct this market research yourself, then you might hire out a third party consultant to help you. Either way, it's important that you get concrete numbers about this.

If you have the initial foresight when you created your business, you can utilize the race, gender, and ethnicity fields in your purchase or application process to create your baseline very easily. For example, if you are planning to penetrate the Hispanic market, you can use your CRM (customer relations management) platform to automatically create a ratio for the amount of business you already receive from the Hispanic market. Work closely with your legal team because in some industries, this might be prohibited.

There are outside research firms that can measure a sample size of your last thousand clients through surnames and other data. For example, they may be able to provide you with information that reveals 5 percent of your total business is already coming from the Hispanic market. While that might sound encouraging, remember that nearly 19 percent of the market is Hispanic. In the example we provided, nearly 45 percent of the Houston market is Hispanic.

Also, the business that's already coming from the Hispanic market might be more of a subconscious competency rather than a conscious strategy. If you're already getting 5 percent of the market subconsciously, imagine what could be with a conscious, targeted strategy. You could become the firm that dominates that market with your product or service.

Do this at the very beginning of your diverse marketing initiative. A year later, you can conduct the same calculation to see how much progress you've made. If you started with 5 percent of your sales coming from the Hispanic market, and you find it's now 10 percent, then the math is made easy.

Of course, you may find that you aren't getting *any* business from your target market with your current efforts. That means your baseline is zero, and you can attribute all of the business you get from the diverse market going forward to your brand new marketing initiative.

MILESTONES TO MEASURE

There are a lot of things you can measure when it comes to your diverse marketing efforts. When it comes to making demonstrable progress along a reasonable timeline, I recommend that you start by focusing on the lower-hanging fruit. Here's a checklist of milestones to consider:

- ☑ In your first week, consider appointing a project manager to help keep you and your team on point.

- ☑ In the first thirty days, complete your secondary research and visit with someone in your desired market.

☑ Within sixty days of that visit, identify key community leaders and connect with them on LinkedIn. Set up meetings with each to learn how to further penetrate the market.

☑ Within the next ninety days, create a segmented value proposition and follow through with it (e.g., revamping your website so it speaks to your target market in a way that communicates that value proposition).

☑ Within 120 days, try to have a hundred LinkedIn contacts of people from your target market. Continue to add more from there.

☑ By day 150, plan to create an email and/or social media campaign that targets the community. Measure the open rate for emails and the clicks and visits to your new website landing page.

☑ By 180 days, you should be measuring the number of sales and new clients that come from your selected market. Six months have passed since you started this initiative, so you should have a good idea of how your efforts are materializing.

☑ By the end of year one, you should be calculating your ROI. Now you can start asking if you're seeing the results you hoped for, and from there, you can decide if you need more capital or if you should adjust your strategy.

☑ With every new year, repeat the last step, adjusting your strategy along the way.

In addition to the checklist, there are some broader market metrics that you may want to keep score of to track your progress.

- *Your communication effectiveness.* Does your team and your company fully support the message you've communicated regarding this initiative? Do they understand that it's one of your key priorities? Have you mentioned this initiative on your website and included it in your company newsletters?

- *Customer satisfaction.* Are your new customers satisfied? It's an achievement to gain a customer in your new market, but will you retain them? How do you reach out to them to check their pulse?

- *Resonating with your new market.* Is your new brand resonating with your new market?

- *Distractions.* Is this initiative distracting from your core business?

- *Project management.* Have you identified a project manager who can assist you and your team in tracking your progress on a weekly and quarterly basis?

- *ROI and metrics.* Are you publishing your ROI and financial metrics regularly to encourage your team?

Once again, it's worth repeating: this is going to take time. The timeline probably makes that clear to you. While this won't take as long as it did when you first created your business, it's still a big, serious move. As you can see, just getting started—getting to a point where you begin to see big ROI—is going to be at least a one-year journey.

You and your team need to thoroughly understand this so you can *hold fast*.

BEYOND THE FACTS AND FIGURES

Although this chapter is one of the shortest in the book, it represents the longest part of your journey into diverse marketing. However, it's also the most exciting because you're going to start seeing your hard work pay off. Your milestones serve as a rain gauge for tracking your progress along the way, and the checklist gives you a clear sense of what exactly you and your team should be working on.

As the opening quote says, what gets measured, gets managed. If you're doing things the right way, with smart planning and a patient allocation of resources, then you are almost guaranteed to see results.

However, there is a side to this success that we haven't discussed yet: the human equation. Anytime you're reaching out to a community, you will be dealing with living, sensitive people who are part of a culture that has been evolving and developing for a very long time. As you stretch yourself to embrace this culture, people will recognize your efforts and appreciate it. And all of this work builds toward a mutual relationship of respect and appreciation between you and your chosen market.

STEP SIX KEY TAKEAWAYS

- The first step in tracking your progress is to create your starting point, or baseline, as an initial reference point. What percentage of your total business is already coming from your target market?

- In order to make demonstrable progress along a reasonable timeline, focus on the lower-hanging fruit from the checklist of milestones in this chapter.

- Measure some broader market metrics as well.

CHAPTER 9

STEP SEVEN: DOING WELL BY DOING GOOD

"We make a living by what we get, but
we make a life by what we give."

—WINSTON CHURCHILL

Consider your original intent when you decided to read this book. Why exactly did you have an initial interest in reaching out to these growing diverse markets? What do you hope to get from it?

Most of the time, when I talk to clients about this, they say they want to drive their top- and bottom-line revenue from a select market—at least, that's their initial goal. However, something interesting occurs when they start to take this journey. As the visionary leader behind the initiative becomes more engrossed in the diverse market, they begin to gain a vision for more than just growing revenue. Their sense of compassion and responsibility for the community takes hold, and gradually, they find that they want to make a positive impact on that community—*doing well by doing good*.

Indeed, the phrase "doing well by doing good" recognizes the capital incentives of your for-profit company but connects it to the good of society. If you can grow your company while, at the same time, making a difference in communities across the country, isn't that a win for everyone?

Yes, you have a revenue goal; there's nothing wrong with that. Far from it. Revenue is how we grow our companies, take care of our teams, and provide amazing products and services. But if you can couple that revenue with a sincere effort to do good for your customers and their communities, all the better. What if doing good actually accelerates your growth?

We have some compelling examples of large companies who are doing just that. Patagonia provides one of the more well-known examples. The eco-friendly, outdoor clothing and equipment manufacturer has become a preferred provider by their environmentally conscious customers due to their demonstrated commitment to sustainability all along the supply chain.

Patagonia is entirely focused on making sure that they have a safe and responsible supply chain, but they also give 1 percent of all sales to environmental groups around the world. Clearly, they have created a profitable business, and they could focus entirely on generating revenue. However, they have chosen to tie their business into something bigger and more significant than simply "doing well." Instead, they choose earnestly to "do good" for the environment and society, and their loyal customers love them for it. It's a win/win!

Believe it or not, Coca-Cola, the iconic soda company, has also taken a similar approach. If you check out the Coca-Cola website and look under the tab labeled "Our Company, " you can navigate to a page that is titled "Sustainability." There, you will find the following declaration: "We act in ways to create a more sustainable and better shared future. To make a difference in people's lives, communities and our planet by doing business the right way."[15]

The page goes on to describes the main tenets of Coca-Cola's commitment to environmental sustainability.

- They commit to making brands and products that people love while building a more sustainable future for their business and the planet.

- They commit to giving consumers more beverage options, including reduced-sugar drinks and smaller packages.

- They aim to collect and recycle one bottle or can for each bottle or can they sell, while making 100 percent of their packaging recyclable.

---

15 "The Coca-Cola Company." 2017. The Coca-Cola Company. 2017. https://www.coca-colacompany.com/sustainability.

- They are committed to water conservation, returning *at least* 100 percent of the water they use in their drinks. In this way, they can increase water security wherever they operate, source ingredients, or touch people's lives.

- They intend to reduce their carbon footprint, with a goal of reducing emissions by 25 percent by 2030.

Environmentally-conscious people have had a strong issue with the millions of cola-filled bottles being pumped into the world every day, but Coca-Cola's efforts to achieve greater sustainability are allowing them to penetrate that market and reclaim lost revenue.

Another great example of doing well by doing good comes from Indeed.com's commercial during the 2021 Super Bowl. Called "The Rising," the commercial targeted a wide range of groups, including numerous minorities. As an article in *Ad Age* explained, "The online job site not only made sure the real job seekers it featured in its first Super Bowl commercial were diverse, but that it was also strategic in how it represented and defined those job seekers. A Black woman is shown getting a job as a software engineer, for example, and a young Black man is called 'experienced.'"[16] Coincidentally, a colleague and good friend of mine, Eszylfie Taylor, is featured in the Super Bowl ad.

Eszylfie Taylor

Jennifer Warren, Indeed's VP of global brand and communications, went on to say, "Inherent in our mission is that we help all people get jobs. I would say it just has always been part of who we are. And when we create our advertising, we make sure to capture and reflect the true labor force and those looking for jobs."

As a result of this ad campaign, many more people from minority groups began using Indeed.com in their

---

16 "Super Bowl LV Advertisers Tackle Diversity, Inclusion with Mixed Results." 2021. Adage.com. February 5, 2021. https://adage.com/article/special-report-super-bowl/super-bowl-lv-advertisers-tackle-diversity-inclusion-mixed-results/2311981.

job searches. While the company no doubt raked in a ton of money by positioning itself as minority-friendly, it did so in a way that made a big difference in the lives of consumers. It generated revenue by connecting employee-seeking companies with minority workers— serving the underserved—and reaped the rewards for doing so. On a grander scale, it also assisted the US in its post-COVID economic recovery and lowered the unemployment rate. Doing well by doing good, indeed.

There are many more examples of this. In 2018, Starbucks made news when they partnered with the organization Feeding America and pledged to donate 100 percent of their leftover food to community groups, simultaneously attacking the problems of national hunger and food waste.[17]

As a final example, we can consider the role that advertising agencies played during the pandemic. When COVID began hitting communities hard, state

17 Barbu, Petra. n.d. "Doing Well by Doing Good: What We Can Learn from 2018'S Most...." Blog.movingworlds.org. September 2021. https://blog. movingworlds.org/doing-well-by-doing-good-what-we-can-learn- from-2018s-most-innovative-companies.

and local governments needed help creating public service announcements, especially ones that targeted diverse segments of the populace that had a higher concentration of the disease. To do that, they turned to numerous ad agencies.

Those ad agencies certainly made a lot of money as a result, but they did so by helping to spread the word about things like vaccinations, booster shots, and important precautions, thus helping to slow the spread of the disease and potentially save lives.

YOUR POTENTIAL IMPACT

There is so much more that companies could be doing if they truly committed to the idea of "doing well by doing good," and they would reap a reward for it. Imagine what a large pharmaceutical company could achieve if they focused their efforts beyond making money and also committed to helping certain underserved demographics. For example, they might focus on selling very affordable blood-pressure medication to markets where high blood pressure is more prevalent.

Of course, they could create a generic value proposition, cast the net widely, and try to get whatever business they happen to get. However, by specifically zeroing in on the African-American community, they could address a particular need in that community while helping to improve the quality of lives of consumers in that market. They would be doing a tremendous amount of good, but they would also reap some well-earned rewards from a grateful community.

A textbook company might decide to focus on educating recent immigrants by offering low-cost courses that teach English as a second language or specific job skills. This education business would profit from diverse marketing while also, at the same time, giving immigrants something that they truly need to raise their economic status.

A financial company could do the same thing by educating immigrants on important American financial products and services that might be unfamiliar to them, like options for funding for education or multi-generational wealth strategies.

Speaking of education, universities often struggle with growing and maintaining enrollment. Many of them offer a variety of programs that support under-served markets, but the people in those segments remain unaware of the available assistance. Imagine how many more people they could reach if they mar-keted effectively to these diverse groups. Not only would they drive attendance and, thereby, revenue, they would also boost education in these underserved markets. Again, doing well by doing good.

I could go on and on with the possibilities. In fact, I believe any company in any industry can find a way to "do well by doing good" to underserved markets. It just requires a bit of creative thinking. So, why don't you make *your company* the next example? Begin thinking of ways you could improve the lives of people in diverse markets while driving revenue by offering your prod-ucts and services.

In the examples I shared, this kind of approach only occurred after visionary company leaders saw what was possible with diverse markets, engrossed them-selves in the culture, and came away with a genuine desire to serve the community. In my experience, this pays off almost every time. And the same principle applies to you. You will do well by doing good. Find an underserved diverse market that will truly benefit from your products and services, learn about their culture, problems, and challenges, and communicate the value of what you have to offer in a way that resonates with them.

The next step in your journey comes once you've done all of this, and you're able to step back and take a look at all you've done, seeing clearly how it worked. You believed me when I talked about the power and opportunity of diverse marketing, but now you know it from personal experience. You have seen the potential, and you know how to harness it.

This experience and knowledge should inspire and empower you to get out there and do it all over again. After all, there are many, many underserved diverse markets just waiting to discover the amazing products and services you have to offer.

STEP SEVEN KEY TAKEAWAYS

- With a bit of creative thinking, any company in any industry can find a way to "do well by doing good" to underserved markets.

- Think of some ways you could improve the lives of people in diverse markets while driving revenue by offering your products and services.

CHAPTER 10

SELECTING YOUR NEXT MARKET

"Momentum begets momentum, and
the best way to start is to start."

—GIL PENCHINA

I love NBA basketball, and my favorite thing is when a player catches a *hot streak* and just starts dominating the court. When a player finds his rhythm and becomes unstoppable. Shot after shot, he grows more confident, each point strengthening the next. It's almost magical. I think about LeBron James scoring sixteen points in two minutes in a game against the Milwaukee Bucks in 2009, or Tracy McGrady scoring thirteen points in thirty-three seconds against the San Antonio Spurs in 2004. There's nothing more thrilling to watch.

By the way, there's real science behind hot streaks. Researchers in the fields of information sciences and operations and decision technologies released the results of a study recently that showed "some players do get consistently 'hot' during games and make more shots than expected following two shots made consecutively."[18] In other words, to put it simply, success begets success. When a player does particularly well, he is inspired to do even better.

I believe that's as true in business as it is in sports. If you have diligently followed the steps laid out in these chapters and executed a well-defined strategy for reaching your selected diverse market, then you should have developed a new revenue stream for your

18 Pelechrinis, Konstantinos, and Wayne Winston. n.d. "The 'Hot Hand' Is a Real Basketball Phenomenon – but Only Some Players Have the Ability to Go on These Basket-Making Streaks." The Conversation. https://theconversation.com/the-hot-hand-is-a-real-basketball-phenomenon-but-only-some-players-have-the-ability-to-go-on-these-basket-making-streaks-179082.

business. You've passionately pursued your vision, and it has changed your life and your business for the better.

By now, your team is probably amazed at what has already been accomplished, and any doubters have either been convinced or scorned. Your competitors are jealous of what you're doing in your target market, and they secretly wish they'd done the work you've done. All they can do now is play a desperate game of catch-up, but you've left them in the dust.

What comes next? First, continue to own and execute on your selected market. Keep developing your diverse marketing strategies to make them even more robust, deepening your reach into the market. Refine your value proposition to attract even more people from your market, and in so doing, make your competition all the more jealous. Solidify your position as the dominant player in that market.

Doing all of this will build momentum and ignite your hot streak. Remember, success begets success. Once you've achieved success in your first market, it's time to double down on your investment by finding your next diverse market to dominate.

Lebron James didn't hit two shots in a row during that famous game in 2009, then throw his hands in the air and say, "Well, I did it. I succeeded! I'm done!" On the contrary, he let the momentum continue to build as he went after another shot, and another, and another. He rode the hot streak as long as he possibly could and crushed the opposing team.

SO, WHO'S NEXT?

So which diverse market will you target next? Will it be based on gender this time? Will you reach out to another ethnicity? Sexual orientation? Religion, perhaps? Personally, I've had a lot of success reaching out to the Asian and Hispanic markets, and I've also had quite a bit of success focusing on specific lifestyle markets in the growing LGBTQ community.

However, I'm currently most interested in the growing Orthodox Jewish market. Just as I've advised you to do, I am immersing myself in that culture, meeting with people, and learning about their unique challenges and issues. Interestingly enough, some of this market is not identifiable through *census.gov* because people in the community simply don't share it with Census takers. Consequently, I can only learn about them through personal observation.

I dived deeper and began to understand their customs and religious traditions. Along the way, as I had suspected, I discovered that there is very little competition in my industry for this market. It was a perfect opportunity to reach out and "do good by doing well." At the time of this writing, I am going through the very steps that I've shared with you in the preceding chapters. I'm developing a specific, targeted value proposition and crafting a strategic plan, even as I think carefully about how I can truly serve this overlooked and underserved community. I've become very aware of the exponential growth in these communities and the huge consumer spending potential that exists.

READY, SET, REPEAT

To select your next diverse market, head back to chapter three and repeat this process all over again. Now that you have an eye for it, you should have an easier time scanning your geographical region for emerging markets. Combine your desire for profit with your desire for doing good for a diverse group, and you will be able to create the same momentum the second time around.

When you really develop a passion for reaching diverse markets, it's going to be evident in everything you do. Customers will sense that passion in the way you communicate the value your company provides. They will see evidence that you and your company genuinely want to know them and serve them, and you will win their business.

As long as you keep moving forward, your hot streak will grow hotter. Before you know it, you'll be starting again with a third diverse market. Then a fourth. And so on.

There are so many growing diverse markets in the country today, and so much untapped potential growth, that you can keep this hot streak going for a long, long time.

THE CHANGING BUSINESS OF AMERICA

"The fact that societies are becoming
increasingly multi-ethnic, multicultural,
and multi-religious is good. Diversity
is a strength, not a weakness."

—ANTONIO GUTERRES

Diversity is a hot topic in the business world, and most
companies have been affected by it in fundamental
ways. In my experience, many of those companies are

dealing with diversity, both internally and externally, in a defensive way rather than being proactive. They pass the "burden" off to human resources or attorneys, or they make token gestures in response to criticism. It's a tremendous missed opportunity.

CEOs need to move from asking, "How do we meet diversity requirements to avoid negative press, litigation, or employee and cultural angst?" to "How can we embrace these diverse cultures and grow our business by serving them?"

Doing that requires visionary leadership. You must be able to see the hidden potential in diverse markets and communicate it powerfully and passionately to your teams, cutting through the resistance of the doubters and naysayers. Visionary leaders understand the advantages of embedding diversity into every aspect of their company's culture, not just in terms of hiring and retention practices but also in regard to marketing and messaging.

Additionally, a visionary leader sees beyond all of the hard work and momentum-building to the possibilities for achieving exponential growth by selecting one diverse market at a time and fully embracing it as a business. Yes, visionary leaders look to the future, but it's important to point out that the changing face of America is *not* the future. It's the present! Diversity is here and now. Realization of the full magnitude of this reality is critical for your team, and it must be up to you to see the vision and encourage all of your people to get fully behind this endeavor.

The effort it will take to develop a new diverse market may be intimidating. That's understandable. And it's going to require that every team member gets on board. The challenge is steep, and some of your team members, even key leaders, will think, "We're already attracting a few diverse customers. There's no need to craft a specific outreach plan for them, is there?"

Anxiety, discomfort with the unknown, and even prejudices are going to create some resistance, but these are obstacles you need to overcome. As you start this journey, it's imperative that all forms of resistance be addressed. Otherwise, it will be very difficult to implement the necessary changes throughout your organization.

Additionally, you need to communicate your vision at every level of your organization, because success isn't going to happen overnight. As a leader, you must understand the timeframe of this endeavor, so you can put all of the hard work into perspective. Remember, this is a years-long commitment that demands patience and diligent execution before you realize massive returns.

Long before that happens, its up to you to conduct secondary research and determine which specific market you believe will be most lucrative. And then, with primary research, you need to familiarize your-self with that market by immersing yourself in it per-sonally, getting to know people in that community, and becoming well acquainted with the language and culture.

There is no substitute for this kind of primary research! If it doesn't come naturally to you, just remind yourself of the long-term opportunity and step boldly out of your comfort zone. The insight you gain from this will play a huge role in identifying your easiest point of entry, as well as creating a specific, segmented value proposition that attracts consumers in your chosen market by speaking to their needs and wishes in their own language.

Indeed, as a visionary leader, you need to play a key role in every aspect of this initiative—from the creation of a marketing plan with key deliverables, timeliness, and financial discipline to the allocation of resources (both financial and human) to reviewing your ROI.

After months of hard work, when some traction has been made in the market and you're beginning to generate real revenue, an interesting phenomenon is going to take place. As success increases, so will your desire to serve the community, and that, in turn, will accelerate your penetration in that market.

When you have a clear sense of how your products and services improve the lives of consumers in the community, it will drive your team further. Your team members will become immersed in the market, too, and all of the "mundane" functions of their ordinary jobs will become part of "doing well by doing good." Every single team member will be driving revenue by changing lives.

Bolstered with confidence, you—as a visionary leader—will see the repeatability of the process, knowing that the next market you choose offers the same benefits as the first. So, off to the next market you will go, even more prepared and confident than you were with the last one. It's a beautiful cycle, building momentum over time and leading you to goal after goal after goal as the hot streak continues as long as you want it to.

Good luck! The opportunity is out there right now. It's massive, and it's just waiting for you to get started.

ADDITIONAL RESOURCES

It's my hope that this book has served you well and set you on the right path into diverse marketing. The initial steps might be a bit intimidating, especially if this is your first time. As you make progress through the steps I've given you in this book, you might come up against some challenges specific to your business, industry, or target market. If you decide that you need additional help or resources to overcome these challenges, I am more than ready to help you become the dominant player in your market. Please reach out to me via my website at *newamericamarketing.com*.

ABOUT THE AUTHOR

Vince Vitiello is a seasoned marketing and sales executive with expertise in the financial services industry. Vince began his career with MetLife as a sales producer. He also led MetLife's marketing and training division at Albany Life in London, England. He has held Chief Marketing and Senior Distribution positions with MetLife, Allianz, and National Life, where he has led career, independent, and broker-dealer sales organizations, both within the United States and internationally.

At MetLife, Vince was responsible for creating and overseeing all Asian distribution in the United States,

turning it into one of MetLife's most profitable segments. Metlife is also where he developed his inextri-
cable dedication to serve multicultural markets. It is
with this intention that Vince started New America
Marketing (NAM) to help larger corporations reach
underserved markets by inducing a catalyst that lives
and breathes diversity.

New America Marketing is a New York-based bou-
tique marketing consulting firm engaged in developing
innovative marketing solutions to help clients achieve
sustainable business growth by leveraging the changing consumer demographic landscape in the country.
At NAM, Vince and his team partner with insurance
firms, financial institutions, and other consumer-fac-
ing companies to help them become more appealing
to the exploding diverse markets.

Vince is also an active board member of the Chinese-American Insurance Association, a member of
the board of trustees for NAIFA (National Association
of Insurance and Financial Advisors), and the President of the board of the Interfaith Nutrition Network
(The INN), which is a charity involved in helping those

affected by hunger, homelessness, and profound poverty on Long Island. Vince lives in New York, with his wife Janet. They have two sons, Matthew and JonPeter.